Con

Aussie
STEM Stars

FIONA WOOD

Inventor of spray-on skin

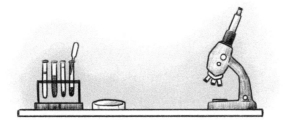

Aussie
STEM Stars

FIONA WOOD

Inventor of spray-on skin

Story told by CRISTY BURNE

WILD
DINGO
PRESS

Aussie STEM Stars series
Published by Wild Dingo Press
Melbourne, Australia
books@wilddingopress.com.au
wilddingopress.com.au

This work was first published by Wild Dingo Press 2020
Text copyright © Cristy Burne

The moral right of the author has been asserted.

Cover Design: Gisela Beer
Illustrations: Diana Silkina
Series Editor: Catherine Lewis
Printed in Australia

Burne, Cristy 1977-, author.
Fiona Wood: Inventor of spray-on skin / Cristy Burne

A catalogue record for this
book is available from the
NATIONAL LIBRARY OF AUSTRALIA National Library of Australia

ISBN: 9781925893281(paperback)
ISBN: 9781925893298 (epdf)
ISBN: 9781925893304 (epub)

Grasp the nettle with both hands and don't let go.

— **Fiona Wood**

Coal village kid

'Who do you think you are?'

The taunt came from behind. Fiona swivelled to see three big boys, taller than her, because, well, who wasn't? She was probably the shortest kid in her class.

Ignore them, she told herself. She readjusted her neatly pressed skirt and schoolbag and kept walking.

The day was grey, a typical Yorkshire morning with ice still shining on some of the puddles. Smoke tumbled from red-brick chimneys atop the two-storey brown-brick houses that lined the street. The walk to school wasn't long, and the cold didn't scare Fiona. She'd been up for hours already, practising.

Athletics Day was coming up. So was her ballet exam, and before breakfast was the best time to sneak a go with Mum's rapiers. They weren't real swords, not really, but it was sprout-picking season, so Mum was gone before first light, not back till after breakfast. Mum's boss said brussel sprouts were sweeter if you picked them in a frost. As if brussel sprouts could taste sweet at all.

Mum had been a champion fencer. She'd been in the Women's Royal Air Force too, after the war. She'd had to lie about her age to get in.

'Think you're better than the rest of us, is that it?' called the biggest boy.

'Too good for Frickley, are you?' called his mate.

The jeering was closer now. Fiona checked the street ahead, scanning for someone who might help. If Geoff and David had been about, it'd at least be an even fight. She quickened her pace.

Too late.

A rock bounced off the back of her schoolbag, another narrowly missed her head. 'You think you're right smart, don't you?'

She could handle their laughter, their jeers, but not rocks being thrown at her head. Not again.

Fiona stopped where she was and turned to glare. All three boy wore school trousers with rumpled shirt collars under mismatched woollen jumpers. They looked mean, shoes scuffed and short hair sticking out like haystacks. Another rock. Fiona dodged.

'What's the matter?' they taunted. 'Scared of a rock?'

'I'm not scared,' she said, keeping her voice steady, even as they came closer. And she wasn't scared, not exactly. More like annoyed. How dare they pick on a little kid? They'd never even try it if her brothers were there. 'Looks to me like you're the scaredy cats. Three of you against one. What's the matter? Scared of me?'

They puffed their chests and stamped their feet, reminding her of grumpy sheep.

'What's that?'

'She calling us scared?'

'She can't do that. Rotten little…'

But Fiona didn't much care what they thought she could and couldn't do. And there was no way

3

she'd let these boys make her late for school. She ran. Quick as you like, they threw their schoolbags to the road and pelted after her, but Fiona was gone.

Faster than the wind. Legs like pistons. Faster and faster. She could hear the horns blast, the crowds roar. A fine start, she'd found her stride. The world record was well within her reach. A sensational final sprint and – yes! The crowds cheered. She smiled for the flashing cameras. A hot favourite for Mexico Olympics, she heard them say. Britain's big hope for bringing home the gold!

'Fiona?' The sound of David's voice broke through her dreaming. 'You alright?'

She looked around, chest heaving and muscles alive. She was at school. She was all in one piece, schoolbag on, no sign of the lads, which meant she'd made it. There was a reason she was an Amateur Athletics Association sprint champion. She flashed David a cheeky grin. 'Alright. You?'

'Alright.' He grinned back, twinkling brown eyes just like his sister's. He was a fast runner, too. The athletics kids called him the Frickley Flyer.

David knew about the bullies. He also knew Fiona could handle them. Between David and

Geoff and baby Nicola, Fiona knew the Wood kids could do anything.

Because in a way, the bullies were right. She did want something better than Frickley. All the Woods did.

There was nothing wrong with Frickley, not really. Her Uncle Cyril had literally never left his village, not even to go five miles down the road, and loads of others were the same. Frickley had an awesome football ground, home to what was surely any-season-now soon-to-be England's number one amateur football team, Frickley Colliery Football Club. Plus, there was the Frickley Colliery Brass Band, that even Grandma admitted was chock-full of talent. And Frickley had a stream to play in and fields to run in and even a super-ancient stone church that Dad said had been around since before the plague. Gruesome!

Best of all, though, it had the coal mine and the farms. Which meant Mum and Dad had jobs, Mum even had two, plus night school, and Dad worked shifts down the pit, just like all the other Frickley dads. Coal dust paid for their clothes, their food, the rent on their pit-owned house. It paid for

Fiona's ballet leotards and Geoff's football boots and David's rugby gear. It had even paid for their first car, a blue-and-white Sunbeam that was the envy of the village.

Fiona sometimes reckoned Dad had paid for it in more ways than one. She could only imagine the darkness of the pit, the falling rock, then Dad crying out and falling still. He'd broken his neck that day. There'd been a payout, but it'd taken him months to recover. He'd never wanted to go down the pit again after that. But it was all he knew how to do, the only way he knew to put food on their table. So, there he was, back down the mine. Fiona knew he hated it, and she knew she never wanted to be trapped like that – with no choice about what she could do and couldn't do in the world.

She could see the mine as she stared outside her classroom window. Its towering pitheads cranked day and night. East and south of here were farms and woodlands. West was the colliery railway and the giant spoil heaps she climbed before and after school, so she could run and run and run.

So it wasn't that there was anything *wrong* with Frickley; it was just that Fiona wanted more. The world was enormous, she knew it, and she wanted to be able to choose what she did in it. Mum and Dad had drummed it into all four of their children.

'You want to be able to get up in the morning and enjoy what you do,' they'd say. 'That means you've got to work hard, so you can make those choices. You've got to train hard, study hard, never give up.'

That night, after homework and athletics practice and helping with tea, Fiona and her brothers left little Nicola with Mum and wandered down to a stretch of bare land near the pit head. They mucked around with a football by the spoil heaps, waiting for Dad and the siren that would signal the end of his shift.

Sometimes, as the sun set and the light and warmth faded from the sky, Fiona tried to imagine living down the mine like the pit ponies. Were they born down there? Or were they led down, on some fateful day when they were still small enough to fit down the shaft, but old enough to work?

Even thinking about it made her feel sick. The low ceilings and never-ending darkness. The heavy, stinking air. The muddy slush of peat coal.

Peat coal

Peat is a low-grade fossil fuel. Soft and crumbly, it forms from dead plants that rot in bogs over many, many years. Peat is the first stage of coal formation. Over time and with enough heat and pressure, peat will eventually form into lignite, known as brown coal.

Fiona tried to imagine her whole life, spent deep beneath the ground, stabled in the dark, hauling tubs of coal to the flats then pulling empty tubs back again, over and over. Pit ponies were bred for the pit. They didn't have a choice. Some might never see the sun's light again.

'Fiona!' a voice called.

She jumped. Dad!

Geoff Wood Senior hadn't had a choice either. He was just 14 when he started full-time down the pit, working as a pony driver. He was a whizz with a football, even won a soccer scholarship to grammar school. But there wasn't money for that. He needed to be earning, helping to support his family, and that meant coal mining. His older brother was already working down the mine.

Pit ponies
Since the 1700s, thousands of horses have worked as pit ponies, hauling heavy tubs of coal along the low, dark tunnels of coal mines and rarely seeing sunlight. The last pit ponies retired in the 1990s. Now machines are used instead.

If you could believe Dad's stories, the Woods had been going down coal mines since Fiona's great, great, great grandfather was killed in one about a zillion years ago. So, when Dad was old enough, Grandma had ripped the studs off his soccer boots – his beloved and only shoes – and he'd walked the same worn track into the darkness and the slush.

Now he was older.

'Hurry up, Fiona!' he called. 'Teatime.'

And moodier, too, Fiona guessed. He was always moody on the days he had to work, which was most of them. Dad had joined the air force after the war, so she couldn't blame him. Who'd want to spend their days in the dark when their dreams were in the sky? Dad had enlisted secretly, to escape the mine … and probably Grandma too, Fiona reckoned. Grandma was a scary woman. She was tall like Dad, and she'd gone off her lolly when she found out he'd gone. And he didn't come back either. At least, not right away. He completed dozens of missions, in exotic places like Singapore and Malaya and India. He'd even played football along the way, for Nottingham Forest, no less. Then one day he'd broken his leg, and so it was back to Frickley, back to crawling around in the dark.

'How was school?' Dad asked, catching each of them in the clear blue of his eyes. 'Working hard? Doing your best?' Dad was a striking man, the sort of soldier they put in tickertape parades. His mates called him Big Geoff and he had the muscles to match. His team had even won the European

Coal Filling Championships. Dad was so big, Fiona wondered how he could even fit down the mine, day after day. Some days, when the twinkle went out of his eyes, she guessed he just didn't.

They walked home together down Westfield Lane, sharing stories and jokes as Dad drilled them on their school lessons. He and Mum made no secret of the fact that they wanted more for their children than mine shafts and frosty sprouts. 'Who am I, not to dream?' Dad would say, when his mates hassled him. But Mum and Dad didn't just dream. They worked, and they made sure their kids did, too.

If Fiona felt disapproving eyes on her family as they walked through town, she gave no sign.

Who cared that the Woods didn't quite fit in? If fitting in meant pretending she dreamed of living all her life in Frickley, then she didn't want to fit in. The Woods all fitted together, they all had big dreams, and Fiona knew exactly what her dreams were. She wanted to be an Olympic sprinter, like Dorothy Hyman and Valerie Peat. Dorothy and Val were coaches at their athletics club. Both came from coal-mining families, both their dads worked down the pit, and look what they had achieved!

So, Fiona was training her guts out, working every morning and afternoon so she could stream across finish lines in Rome and Tokyo and maybe even as far away as Perth, Australia, where Dorothy Hyman had won gold not once but twice! One look at them running and Fiona knew they loved what they did. They jumped out of bed in the morning, eager to get started. They were living proof that nothing was impossible, not if you worked at it long enough.

At least, that's what Fiona thought then.

2

Don't mess with Fits

No matter how fast the other kids hurled insults, Fiona knew she could run faster. Meet day for Athletics Club was coming up and Fiona was planning to win the 100-metre sprint, again.

'You're only as good as your last race,' Dad told her. So she was practising after school three times a week, running around and around the Club's purpose-built cinder tracks.

She'd been so busy training, she hadn't seen the school bullies in days. Or maybe they'd finally decided to leave her alone. That could happen, right?

Then one day, she spotted them in the lanes outside school. They'd gathered in a semicircle around the smallest girl in the class. Fiona's heart sank. The little girl was even younger than Fiona, a thin child with a thin face, ragged clothes and straggly hair. The girl wasn't exactly friends with Fiona, but she wasn't not-friends either. She just sort of *was*. The kind of girl who seemed to shrink in the spotlight if it ever pointed her way.

And it was pointing her way right now.

'Where are your shoes?'

'You can't call those things shoes.'

'What's the matter? Can't Mam buy you proper clothes?'

The three of them took turns shoving her, pushing her like a doll till she was backed against the laneway fence.

Fiona ran. By the time she'd busted in on their little triangle, the girl had cried wet lines down her dusty face.

'Get away from her!' Fiona stood between her and the boys, both her fists up. She figured this wasn't the time for running. No, this was a time for fighting, the kind of time Dad and Sailor Smith always talked about.

Sailor Smith lived in the old folks' home across the road. He didn't look like a fighter. He was tiny and wiry and wrinkled all over, more like someone's grandpa than a boxer. He had to be the oldest person Fiona knew, older even than Grandma, with short, grey hair and the most enormous ears Fiona had ever seen. Cauliflower ears, he called them, and that's exactly what they looked like.

You got cauliflower ears from being hit in the head, Geoff said. And you got hit in the head from being a fighter.

Cauliflower ears
Cauliflower ears are caused by damage to the outer ear. When you're hit about the head, skin can separate from cartilage and blood clots can form, cutting off blood supply to parts of your ear. This causes lumpy white scars that look like cauliflowers. In the past, you could recognise many boxers and rugby players by their cauliflower ears. Today, athletes often wear headgear to protect their ears.

Sailor Smith had been a professional fighter once. 'Super-bantam division,' he'd tell them, over tea. 'Wasn't doing too badly, either, till the Germans started up with their war.'

After World War One he never really went back into boxing. Now he popped over sometimes to borrow a cup of sugar. More often, Dad and the boys popped over for training. Dad had been a street fighter, too, as a lad. Sailor Smith had trained him then, and he trained all three Wood men now.

But not Fiona. 'A fight's no place for a girl,' Sailor Smith would say.

But that didn't seem fair. Seemed to Fiona like it wasn't up to Sailor Smith, or Dad, or anybody else to decide what her place might be. Seemed to her, getting good at something was just a matter of how hard she was prepared to work at it. So, work at it she did.

Sailor Smith couldn't stop her watching their training sessions. She'd sit there, in her dance leotards with ringlets and a lollipop. And then, when she was alone with her brothers, she'd try out what she learned. And as for real-world experience? Well, dealing with louts was always good for a bit of hands-on development.

'What? You going to fight us all?' the ringleader jeered now, looking to his friends for encouragement.

Fiona doubled up her fists, heart going a million miles an hour. 'If I have to.'

'You can't,' they laughed.

She didn't even bother to roll her eyes. Here it was again. Somebody who thought they knew what she could and couldn't do. 'Are you going to leave her alone or what?'

The ringleader stepped forward, shoving Fiona squarely in the chest. She staggered back beneath

his weight. But in that moment something hardened in Fiona. Oh no you don't, she decided.

Enough was enough.

She charged.

Using both arms as battering rams, she smashed into shoulders, stomach, chest. She was quick on her feet; ballet was good for that. And she screamed blue murder as she charged, aiming jabs with her elbows, twisting and kneeing, scratching and clawing. You'll not mess with me again, she thought. You'll not mess with me, or anyone else who's littler or weaker than you. You'll never do this again.

The ferocity of her attack took them by surprise. The ringleader got in a few punches, half-heartedly at first, then for real as he realised this girl was fighting to win. One punch knocked Fiona squarely in the chin, but she hardly felt it. When eventually they stepped back, she let them. They stood there, puffing and staring as if she were some sort of freak.

She faced them all, fists up and panting. 'Giving up already? Come on then, who's next?'

The first boy shook his head and cringed away.

'You're crackers,' he told her. 'She's mad,' he told his mates. 'Like she's having a fit or something.'

Fiona stood there, fists still up and heart beating hard. She watched as they turned on their heels and retreated down the lane towards school. No one wanted to fight a wild thing. Well, good.

She watched them leave. Then she wiped the sweat and hair from her face, allowed herself to relax. 'Are you okay?' Fiona asked. The little girl nodded, gratefully, and Fiona grinned. 'They won't bother us again. Come on, we don't want to be late.'

After that, the lads never troubled Fiona again. In fact, they gave her a new nickname, to match her new reputation. 'Don't mess with Fits,' they'd say, 'or she'll go at you like you wouldn't believe'.

Over the years, Fiona defended others, fighting back against bullies many times. Little did she know she would one day be dealing with the consequences of violence as a regular part of her job. She'd need to find other ways of dealing with the bullies who stood in her way.

3

Not university material

That night, Fiona set the table with some of the dozens of cross-stitched table mats she'd sewed at school. Most kids made one or two, but Fiona had made dozens, enough to wallpaper the whole house, Mum reckoned. 'Perhaps it's time to focus on something else now, dear,' Mum said, eventually.

But it made no difference. Whatever Fiona set her mind to, she did with all her heart. She wanted to be the club's fastest runner and the dance school's prima ballerina and also the school's best needleworker. 'You can take pride in a job well done,' Dad used to say. And Fiona did.

Over supper of stew and potatoes, five of the six Woods chatted about their days. The boys talked rugby training and football, Nicola showed off some impressive gravel burns – her first attempt at hurdles – and Dad mostly listened. Mum was already at work. Most nights she was a youth worker, helping kids and families who lived with disadvantage.

When Fiona thought about where her parents had come from, how hard they both had to work each day, it seemed they were also living with disadvantage. Anytime Fiona wasn't in the mood for maths or spelling, she just pictured Mum, digging sprouts in the frosty dark. Or Dad, working eight-hour shifts in the airless dark, a mile under the ground.

'Grab the nettle with both hands,' Mum would say. 'It may sting, but if you don't grab it, the chance will pass you by.'

The whole idea of voluntarily putting her hands on a stinging plant was slightly odd, but Fiona got Mum's drift. If ever an opportunity came her way, she grabbed it. She took to everything like a bull at a gate, and that included school. Mum and Dad hadn't been able to finish school. Their families were so poor they'd had to get full-time jobs, aged just 12 and 13, to earn money to help buy food and pay bills.

But Fiona didn't have those pressures.

She never dreamed she wouldn't get the chance to finish high school. By the time Fiona was in Grade 6, her brother David was already on the fast-track to university. He'd aced his Eleven Plus exams and won a spot in a selective grammar school. Mum and Dad almost burst with pride just thinking about it.

Eleven Plus exam
The Eleven Plus exam was used in England to test what high school kids could go to. There were three types of high school: grammar, secondary modern or technical. Only kids who won a spot in a grammar school could go on to university, so your future was decided when you were just eleven years old.

Even Geoff, who'd left school in Year 10, was still studying, still rolling up to night school, night after night, clinging tightly to his dream of studying law at Cambridge University. Cambridge! Fiona could almost hear the villagers scoff. As if Frickley's Geoff Wood, who'd struggled at school all his life, would ever get into a university like Cambridge. Geoff couldn't even pass his Eleven Plus, let alone gain entrance to one of England's most prestigious tertiary institutions.

But Fiona never doubted her brother would get there. Just as she never doubted she'd have a chance to follow in her brothers' footsteps.

But then, far away in London, inside the buildings of British Parliament, a new law was passed. Fiona didn't know it then, but Britain was rolling out a nationwide change to the public education system. A change that meant she and Nicola would soon find themselves in a difficult situation.

Meanwhile, Fiona's life continued, oblivious to the challenges in her future.

On the morning she ran and lost her 400-metre race, Fiona realised two things: one, she had trained non-stop, given it her all, and it hadn't been enough. And two: she couldn't give up. She thought of Valerie Peat, sprinting to gold with her waist-length hair streaming behind her. She imagined herself being interviewed for TV, wearing the tracksuit that said *Great Britain*.

Was there ever a time you considered giving up on your dream? the interviewer would say, holding the microphone to Fiona's happy face.

Many times, she'd say. But those were the times I knew I had to step up. I needed to try harder.

So, try harder she did. On the days she wasn't practising at the club, she ran up and down the mine's slag heaps, building her strength, building her resilience in the steaming cold winter mornings. Valerie Peat and Dorothy Hyman had done it, and that made everything possible.

Mum and Dad stepped up, too. Dad traded the family's blue-and-white Sunbeam for a bigger car, wide enough to fit all four kids across the single back seat.

'It's a Humber Super Snipe,' he announced proudly, holding the passenger door open so Mum could slide into the front seat. 'We can drive the kids to Doncaster now.'

Doncaster was ten miles from Frickley, and posher, too. They had a better athletics club at Doncaster, with access to proper coaches and regular competitions across all of Yorkshire. The Humber Super Snipe meant Fiona could now compete against the best runners in Yorkshire. From that moment on, Mum and Dad were in and out of that car every Tuesday, Wednesday and

Friday night, plus all weekend, every weekend, driving the Wood tribe to their various sporting activities.

'And you want to know the best thing about it?' asked Dad, giving Mum one of his rare cheeky grins.

'What?' asked Mum.

'It's an ex-taxi,' said Dad. 'Watch.'

Fiona caught his twinkling eye in the rear vision mirror as he hit the button. From the middle of the car, a wall of glass appeared, separating the front seat from the rear seat.

'What the…?' said Geoff.

Fiona could only gape. It was like some sort of spy-car. And up in front, insulated from their rowdy kids by a wall of soundproof glass, Mum and Dad were laughing. Fiona laughed too, and the kids spent their car trips happily rolling around on the bench seat in the back. 'We can make as much noise as we like!' David hooted, and so they did.

The Woods were the first on their street to own a television set, and by now NASA's Space Program was in full swing. Astronauts were being chosen and trained, some were even blasting into space, orbiting Earth in Gemini spaceships, and much of it was being reported on TV. At nights, Fiona would stare out of her bedroom window, imagining herself up there, far above the confines of the mining village, flying through an endlessness of stars.

NASA space program
In the 1960s, NASA's space program really took flight! The first American to orbit Earth, John Glenn, blasted off in 1962. Project Mercury and Project Gemini flew more than a dozen missions over the next few years. Then the Apollo program began, and on July 20, 1969, Neil Armstrong stepped onto the moon for the first time.

Then, on Thursday, 3 June 1965, Fiona witnessed NASA's live launch. James McDivitt and Ed White climbed onboard Gemini IV and were blasted into space on live TV. Watching this in the lounge room, Fiona felt a thrill run through her. She still wanted to compete at the Olympics, but now she had discovered another electrifying goal.

'Mum,' she announced. 'I'm going to be the first woman to land on the moon.'

And watch out anyone who tried to say she couldn't.

Mum didn't dismiss Fiona's dream. But, unbe-known to Fiona, she was already fighting for it.

Months earlier, Mum had written a letter to the Education Minister at the Department of Education in London. In her letter, she'd outlined her family's situation: Because of the school catchment they lived in, Fiona and Nicola had no way to continue their education beyond Year 10. In their area, there was no school offering free education through to Years 11 and 12. The new education system meant there just wasn't an option that would see them through to university. Was there anything that could be done…?

But earlier that week, Mum had received a letter back.

The letter has been long-since lost, but its message was clear:

Dear Mrs Wood,

Thank you for your correspondence. We appreciate your concern for your daughters' education. I'm sure they are very good people. However, it's not worth sending Fiona and Nicola to university. We feel they're just not university material.

Not university material?

The very thought was impossible. While Fiona continued to shoot for the moon, Fiona's mum began to look for another way.

An
Ackworth kid

Four miles down the road – and a thousand miles from what could be expected for someone growing up opposite the pit – was a school. Ackworth School, it was called, one of England's most expensive boarding schools.

Fiona sometimes saw Ackworth kids around town. They always looked so happy and smartly dressed. They wore navy skirts with blue-and-white striped shirts and the most gorgeous navy cloaks, with pale blue lining in the hood. Oh, to wear one of those cloaks.

Ackworth hadn't always been a school. Back in the 1700s, more than 250 years before Fiona was born, it'd been a home for orphans. Foundlings, they called them. Babies no one wanted, babies no one else could take.

Now it was a co-ed boarding school run by Quakers, whatever they were. And so expensive there was no way Fiona could even think of stepping through its gates, let alone wearing one of their cloaks. On a coal miner's salary? Not in a million years.

Quakers
Quakers belong to the Society of Friends, a religion which began in England in the 1650s. Quakers believe each individual is responsible for developing their own understanding of God.

But astronauts needed a university education. So, Mum needed a way for Fiona and Nicola to stay at school. Because if her children couldn't dream, how could they know what to aim for?

Fiona noticed something strange about Mum at breakfast. She always liked to dress well, making sure their clothes were freshly laundered and pressed. But today, she'd taken extra care with her hair, put extra polish on her shoes.

'Where are you off to, then?' Fiona asked.

'A job interview,' Mum replied. Which struck Fiona as odd. Mum already worked mornings and nights and cooked and cleaned and went to night school. How would she squeeze in another job?

'What job?'

'At Ackworth,' Mum said. And Fiona's heart leapt. But Mum wasn't a schoolteacher. She was a youth worker. A fruit picker. 'What sort of job?' Fiona asked.

'Housemother,' said Mum, looking a little nervous.

'What's a housemother?'

Mum helped herself to another slice of toast. 'Not sure,' she admitted. 'But this is a house, and I'm a mother.' She dusted the crumbs off her hands. 'Seems to me I'm perfectly qualified.'

So that morning, Mum caught the bus four miles into the next town to have her interview. That whole day at school, Fiona could hardly bear to think about it. If her mum got a job at Ackworth, then maybe, just maybe, the school might let her and Nic attend for free.

When Mum reported back to her family that night, she looked exhausted. The interview had lasted an entire two hours.

'Did you get the job?' they asked excitedly. 'Are you going to be a housemother?'

Mum shook her head.

Fiona felt her dream slip away. 'That's okay, Mum,' she said. 'There'll be other jobs.'

But Mum wasn't looking sad. She was grinning like a cat in cream. 'I missed out on housemother because … they want me to be the new Phys Ed teacher!'

Fiona literally danced around the table. A Phys Ed teacher? How could that even be? Mum didn't have any formal qualifications. But she'd somehow made it happen. Fiona felt like pinching herself.

'There's a schoolhouse for all of us to move into,' Mum continued. 'Four bedrooms, right at the school gates. I'll work five days a week, starting the first Monday of next term.' She turned to Dad. 'We can give notice at this place and move in over the summer.'

'And the girls?' he asked, eyes twinkling.

Fiona held her breath.

Mum's smile took up most of her face. 'They can attend Ackworth as staff children,' she said. 'If they want to.'

And in that moment, Fiona's life changed forever. 'Oh, Mum,' she sighed. 'I'd love to!'

In the weeks that followed, Fiona learned that Quakers were a religious group. They called themselves The Society of Friends, which Fiona thought was a good sort of a name. Her school in the village had been less about having friends and more about staying alive.

She packed the last of her belongings into the Super Snipe and the Woods drove away from their pit cottage for the last time. She felt something heavy lift from her shoulders.

But attending Ackworth as a staff child wasn't going to be easy, at least not as easy as Fiona had hoped. For a start, staff children weren't exactly free.

'Thirty pounds?' Fiona gasped, hardly believing. 'But that's…'

Thirty pounds was so much she could hardly bear to think of it. Would her parents really invest thirty pounds sending her to school?

'Thirty pounds *each*, for you and for Nicola, every year,' nodded Mum. 'And the school won't tolerate nonsense from the child of a teacher. And you'll have to give up a few things, too. We won't be able to head off to Doncaster three times a week, for a start. You'll have to train yourselves if you want to compete.'

None of it mattered. Fiona was off to Ackworth!

The Wood's new rental house was a mess. Covered in dust, it'd once been a shop, but not for at least fifty years, Fiona thought. It was the end house in a terrace of five or six houses, all designed in 1820 by some architect who'd apparently been the bee's knees. Now, it looked like somewhere spiders went to die.

'Spooky, isn't it?' Nicola whispered, holding her big sister's hand as they peered into what would soon become their living room.

'Very,' Fiona whispered back. There was something in this room, she couldn't be sure what, but she didn't like it.

In later years, during her time at medical school, Fiona would sometimes return to this house for the holidays. If ever she had to spend the night there alone, she'd take Mum's fencing swords to bed with her, stashing them carefully under the bed in case she needed protection from ghosts.

But on this day, Fiona couldn't imagine spending a single night in this house, let alone the rest of her schooling years.

'Nothing a bit of hard work won't fix up,' declared Dad, staring in at the old storeroom, which was heaped with dusty boxes and cans and all manner of jumble. 'It's got good bones.'

Fiona felt like skeletons might still be buried somewhere in the house's 'good bones'. She shivered just walking through the door. The place was built entirely of stone, with high ceilings and big Georgian-style windows.

'Why are the windows all barred?' she asked.

'They're not bars,' Mum said impatiently. 'That was the fashion back then.'

'Saved on glass,' said Dad with a wink.

Over the summer holidays, Dad called up some mates from the mine and everyone put their shoulder to the wheel. Slowly, day by day, the dusty shop became a family home.

'Geoff and David can have a room each,' Mum declared. 'Fiona and Nic, you'll share this room.' She sighed happily. 'No more getting up at the crack of dawn to pick sprouts.' She was going to be a teacher now!

Everyone helped get the house ready. When Fiona wasn't scrubbing and painting and digging out the new veggie patch, she was working in the fields, earning pocket money by picking peas. Or playing in what the Wood kids called their secret garden: a courtyard of trees to climb and nooks to explore, all hidden away behind the row of houses.

The night before their first day at school, Fiona and Nicola stayed up extra late, whispering in the dark.

What would it be like at Ackworth? Would they have to fight other kids, just to be themselves? Would they make any friends at the Society of Friends?

'Grasp the nettle with both hands,' Mum had said, kissing the girls goodnight. 'Some days it will hurt to hold on, some days you'll need help to hold on, but when opportunities like this come by, there's no question, you have to hold on.'

I will, thought Fiona. I will grab this chance and I won't ever let go.

That night, as she lay in bed, trying not to worry, trying to sleep, she knew she had to be prepared for anything. Fights, bullies, rejection, failure. Mum getting this job was the biggest opportunity of Fiona's life, there was no doubt about it.

So, whatever happened tomorrow, whatever future Ackworth might bring, she'd work and work to make the most of it.

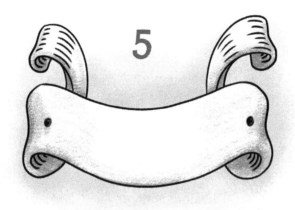

Non sibi sed omnibus

After breakfast one morning in 1971, Fiona walked through Ackworth's big wrought-iron gates for the first time. Almost at once, the school felt different. Everything was polished flagstones and hushed tones, manicured gardens and those gorgeous, gorgeous cloaks. Even the school motto was different.

'*Non sibi sed omnibus*,' Fiona read, fumbling over the Latin. *Not for oneself, but for all.* Which sounded okay in theory...

She walked across the football-field-sized lawn, searching for her homeroom. She didn't know a soul, but it seemed most of the kids already knew each other. They walked in twos and threes, talking quietly. She waited for a fight to break out, for someone to swear or punch or yell. But nothing happened. Curious.

Right from her very first class, Fiona sat in the front row. In her old school, she'd been teased for sitting there, the front row was for nerds, but who cared what other kids thought of her? Fiona had her sights set on becoming an astronaut, and Mum had made it very clear: if Fiona wanted to go to university, she'd need to win a scholarship. There just wasn't enough money.

So, where better to sit than the front row? I'm only going to get one chance at this, she thought.

Just minutes later, after homeroom began, she'd made her first friend.

'Sorry I'm late.'

Standing at the front door, with a late note and a cheeky grin, was a girl with long brown hair.

'Miss Harris,' said the teacher disapprovingly. 'Late on your very first day?' Fiona braced for a dressing down. Instead, the teacher merely gestured. 'Please take a seat.'

Jane Harris slid in next to Fiona. 'Alright?' she whispered at Fiona, grinning.

'Alright,' said Fiona.

'Now, if we're all ready,' the teacher said, 'welcome back to Ackworth, ladies and gentlemen. It's wonderful to see so many familiar faces, and some new faces, too.' She gave Fiona a warm smile.

'Our aim today is to see everyone smoothly into their first week. Those of you interested in sport, music, drama or community service, there are lists going up outside the library. Please add your name if you wish to join.'

'I'm joining everything!' Jane winked at Fiona.

Fiona stared, surprised at her friendliness. 'Me too,' she decided.

Turned out Fiona and Jane were in the same schoolhouse: Gurney. There was also Woolman, Penn and Fothergill.

Dr John Fothergill
John Fothergill was born in Yorkshire in 1712. He was a Quaker scientist and medical doctor who trained at St Thomas's Hospital in London (just like Fiona would years later!). He loved growing plants and learning about plant species. He also worked to improve conditions for the poor, children, prisoners and slaves. He was the founder of Ackworth School, a school that aimed to teach children to help others.

It wasn't long before Jane and Fiona were best friends. Jane and her older brother Nick had been boarding at Ackworth since Grade 8. Jane's parents and her grandparents were Quakers, so they'd all been to Ackworth for generations. Which meant that unlike Fiona, Jane wasn't all that in love with the school. And unlike Fiona, Jane didn't really care if she stayed or not. She did exactly as she pleased, and Fiona couldn't help admiring her.

Soon, Fiona was walking the fine line between being a teacher's kid and being the school rebel's best friend. She wanted to make the most of every opportunity Ackworth gave her, even the ones that meant breaking the rules.

Some nights Fiona and Jane would sneak in treats and have midnight feasts in Jane's room, just like in the novels Fiona liked to read. They'd scoff chocolate and Coke and crisps and tell ghost stories in the creaking, groaning darkness. Jane didn't care if they were caught; she didn't even care about her marks. But Fiona wanted both: midnight feasts *and* a scholarship to university.

She poured herself into every day. She joined the hockey team, the basketball team, the athletics team. She tried slalom canoeing, which turned out to be racing canoes up and down river rapids, complete

> **Eskimo roll**
> Capsised your kayak? No worries. Just bend, flick your hips, swish your paddle and voila! You're flipped back up the right way, and all without having to exit your boat.

with eskimo rolls and trick dives. What a blast! Her coaches focused on teamwork and excellence, her teachers emphasised tolerance and independent thinking.

But the more things Fiona tried, the more she began to realise she couldn't master everything. She'd have to choose.

Fiona was still running on the school team, still practising in the fields many mornings, but she just wasn't getting any faster. Maybe – and this killed her to admit – but just maybe she was as fast as she was ever going to get.

A few years ago, she'd believed hard work would be enough. Now she began to realise that hard work was essential, but it wasn't everything. It was time to face facts. She'd stopped growing at just 157 centimetres tall. She was fast, no doubt, but she'd never be fast enough to pay her bills with running.

Being an astronaut, though, now that was still an option.

Fiona began to focus on her studies. Chemistry, physics, maths, everything a good astronaut would need. Her teachers were passionate and excited by their subjects, and Fiona caught their excitement. Slowly but surely, without ever intending to, Fiona began to develop a following at the school. She wasn't *popular* exactly. She didn't have loads and loads of friends. It was more that she never tried to please the crowd; she just did what needed to be done, and other kids were swept along by her courage. When Fiona studied in the library, others went to study, too. When the basketball team needed a captain, Fiona's teammates voted her in. She even found herself elected to the school council. She couldn't believe her luck. Not only did this school encourage its students to stand up and speak out for what they believed in, it valued what they said.

Well, most of the time.

At one meeting, the entire student council was caught up in a long discussion about school uniforms. The headmaster wasn't keen on sleeveless jumpers and he lectured on and on about it for long and dreary minutes. Forty long and dreary minutes, in fact. Eventually, after everyone was bored silly by all the energy given to this one tiny detail, the headmaster turned his attention to the last item on the agenda.

'Soup and Salad Day,' he read. 'Right then, so...'

Soup and Salad Day was run by the student council. They organised a soup-and-salad meal and anyone who wanted to eat it paid a couple of pounds. All the money went to charity. Soup and Salad Day had been a big part of the school's calendar in previous years, and Fiona was hoping to run it this year. But it was not to be.

'Noble as Soup and Salad Day might be,' the headmaster said, 'we must acknowledge that it involves a lot of time and work and really puts the kitchen staff out as well. I'm afraid it may be time for us to reconsider its place in our timetable.'

Fiona gaped.

'Now, given how late this meeting is running, I propose that for this year, we give Soup and Salad Day a miss. Were there any other matters before we bring this meeting to a close?'

Fiona couldn't stand it. She jumped to her feet. 'With due respect, sir, I'd like to continue discussing the previous matter.'

'But we're out of time,' said the headmaster.

And why was that? 'Sir, you've kept everybody in this room for forty minutes discussing whether or not we can wear sleeves, and the one thing we

can do for others, you've dismissed in just two minutes.'

Fiona swallowed hard. 'I'm afraid I don't think that's appropriate.'

Well, you could've heard a pin drop.

Nobody breathed.

Everyone knew it was true. Wasn't that the motto of the school? *Not for oneself, but for all.* Didn't Ackworth encourage its students to serve their community, not bicker about fashion?

There was a long and tense pause.

'On reflection,' announced the headmaster, 'we will continue to explore opportunities to support our charitable causes.'

After the meeting, the other councillors gathered around Fiona.

'Weren't you scared?' they asked her.

Fiona shook her head. 'Mostly irritated. Imagine wasting all our time and then cancelling a charitable event to boot. That's absolutely inappropriate.'

'I could never have done it,' said one student.

Fiona turned to her. 'But you must,' she said passionately. 'It's so much worse to do nothing. What happens if we all do nothing? We just go back to our rooms and complain? That's a waste of everyone's time. Each of us is responsible for standing up and saying something.'

That set the other kids squirming. 'It's just so hard...'

'I know it's hard,' Fiona said, 'but the more of us who do stand up, the easier it becomes.'

When the time came for staff and students to vote for Head Girl, Fiona won by a mile.

But even being Head Girl wasn't enough to protect her.

6

Silence
in the library

Fiona was still dedicated to her studies, spending many lunchtimes and free periods in the library. It was in the library that her dreams of making it to university faced their biggest threat yet.

The school library was a beautiful building, with rich mahogany doors, old-fashioned chandeliers and shelves and shelves of books. It even smelled like a library. It sounded like one, too. SILENCE IN THE LIBRARY read a sign at the door.

One afternoon, Fiona and a bunch of other kids were at the library, studying in silence. The door banged and a kid came scrambling noisily through the door, followed equally noisily, by a member of staff.

The previously quiet library began to echo with the sound of a stern telling-off. The teacher went on and on, loudly listing the ways in which his student had disappointed.

Fiona looked around. Not a single kid was studying. But still, the conversation continued.

She put down her pencil.

'Excuse me, sir,' she said quietly.

The teacher looked her way.

'We're trying to work,' Fiona explained calmly. 'There's a sign on the door just there. It says silence in the library. And I do believe that means everyone.'

Yikes. Even for a school like Ackworth, where students and teachers were encouraged to give everyone's voice an equal space, Fiona's observation was incredibly brave. But she spoke up anyway. She wanted the chance for everyone to study in silence.

But the teacher didn't see it that way. He thought Fiona's comments were rude.

The case quickly escalated, and before she knew what was happening, Fiona was justifying herself to the entire school. There were meetings. Debates. Full-on mediation. Many people agreed with Fiona. Many agreed with the teacher.

And if the school decided that Fiona was in the wrong, what would happen next? Would she have to resign as Head Girl? Would she lose her position as a staff child? Could she even be expelled? She didn't know. But she didn't give up.

It was inappropriate, she explained, for anyone – especially a teacher – to be so loud in the library. The school library should be a refuge for study and quiet thought.

In the end, Fiona's arguments won through. The school decided that everyone, even teachers, should respect the library's silence. Fiona stayed at the school and kept her position as Head Girl.

All that week at Daily Worship, Fiona marvelled at how lucky she was to be at a school where the voices of kids counted as much as the voices of adults.

Daily Worship was an Ackworth tradition, a short silence before every meal and at school assembly, too. Once a week there was an even longer silent time, called Meeting for Worship. It wasn't really worship. You didn't have to pray or anything. You just had to sort of sit and think. Be mindful, maybe. There weren't even any real rules about what to think, and that suited Fiona just fine. She'd usually spend this time staring out the window at trees and clouds, thinking of anything she liked. Brilliant.

And now she thought of how important it is to make space for everyone's voice, to give everyone's opinion a place at the table.

Over many years, Fiona never lost this respect for other voices. In leading teams through challenge after challenge, she realised that everyone had something special to offer. Sometimes honesty was what was needed. Sometimes loyalty. And always a good dose of courage.

7

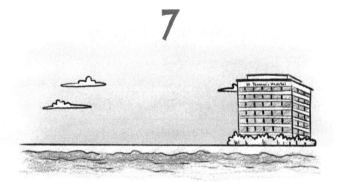

One of the
Tommy's crew

Fiona shoved a pillow over her head. How do you even decide what you want to do for the rest of your life?

First it had been sprinting, then astronaut training. Now, after giving 110 per cent all through school, Fiona thought she'd finally settled on what she really wanted to do. Physics and maths. At Cambridge University.

While at Ackworth, she'd discovered she loved science, the thrill of understanding something new, the way every piece of knowledge only led to more questions.

'I just worry you won't be able to support yourself,' Mum said, sitting on Nicola's bed opposite Fiona. 'How will science and maths pay your bills? You want to be independent, don't you?'

Fiona pulled the pillow off, stared out her window at the scudding clouds. Of course, she wanted to be independent. But back in the 1970s, nobody really knew what scientists and mathematicians even did. Teacher was a job. Doctor was a job. Even astronaut was a job. But what exactly was a scientist?

'But I *like* science,' Fiona insisted. And she did. Inventions. Discoveries. New knowledge of the world. She couldn't get enough.

'You can still study physics and maths if you're at Tommy's,' Mum tried. 'Plus, you'll have David there, to look out for you. I'm sure doctors use physics and maths all the time.'

Fiona wasn't so sure. David had been studying medicine at the prestigious St Thomas's Hospital Medical School for two years already, but he'd wanted that since forever. Even as a little boy, he'd always wanted to be a doctor.

Yet Mum had a point. One look at the newspaper showed it. There were plenty of jobs for doctors, but back then there weren't many jobs for physicists and mathematicians.

And jobs were especially valuable. Miners all over England were striking for better conditions, better pay. But all they were getting was fired. Even Dad had lost his job. He and his mates were now working for Fiona's big brother, Geoff, in a shopfitting business. Better than being down the mine, but not quite what Fiona had in mind.

'Why not go to London?' Mum suggested. 'Go and visit David, see Tommy's, see if you like it. You've done well in your exams. You'll probably get the marks to study medicine. Why not go have a look, see if you like it?'

It was tempting. London! Fiona hadn't spent much time in the city, and she hadn't seen David in ages. But she still wasn't convinced.

Then Geoff poked his head around the door.

'I'll take you,' her big brother offered. 'Just you and me and David, we'll have a weekend in London.'

Mum opened her mouth, but shut it again when she saw Fiona's face.

A whole weekend in London. With both her brothers... Even if she didn't like Tommy's, that sounded like a whole lot of fun.

Fiona never imagined how much fun.

St Thomas's Hospital Medical School
St Thomas's Hospital was named in 1173 for Saint Thomas Becket, an Archbishop who was murdered by King Henry II's knights, three years earlier. The hospital began as a sick house where monks and nuns treated the sick and needy for free. Nearly 850 years later, it is a thriving and world-renowned public hospital. The St Thomas's Hospital Medical School was established in 1550 and is still one of the world's most prestigious.

St Thomas's itself, though, was massively intimidating. Huge, right opposite the British Parliament, right on the River Thames. And posh as. The building was ten storeys high at least, a brown monolith of a thing. Fiona counted ten windows across every storey. How would she ever learn her way around? Cold wind from the river whipped along the street and Fiona shivered. Could she really thrive here?

'Don't worry, sis,' joked David, punching her arm, 'they've been training doctors here for hundreds of years. I bet they can even train you.'

With wobbly legs, Fiona followed Geoff and David into the shadow of the building. The whole place stank like a … hospital. But she liked the busyness of it. The uniforms, the urgent air. She liked the fact that there were people here she could help. Wasn't that what medicine was all about?

That weekend was quite the party. David introduced Fiona and Geoff to loads of his friends, all second-year med students living it up in the city. There was music, dancing, food and fashion. They all seemed so hip, so sure of themselves. Fiona suddenly felt sure she could handle this med student life.

She changed her university preferences as soon as she arrived home. All that stood between her and a new life in medicine was the St Thomas's Medical School entrance interview.

Fiona could only hope she was ready.

When the time came, the interview room was larger than she'd expected, with wooden panelling on the walls and a huge wooden desk behind which sat two men wearing suits and ties. Fiona smoothed the hem of her skirt.

'Miss Wood,' said the first one, an elderly man with a grey beard and grey eyes. He gestured at a chair that sat conspicuously empty on Fiona's side of the desk. 'Have a seat.'

The interview began almost at once. Sit straight, Fiona told herself. Pay attention. This is your chance. Maybe your only chance.

The first introduced himself as the Dean of the School; the second man, with piercing eyes, was the Professor of Anatomy.

Fiona answered questions about her grades and her hobbies, tried to control the wobble in her throat. Think positive. Hang on.

The dean looked down at her over the rim of his glasses as he scanned her application.

'Head girl, very good. Basketball captain. Hmm. And slalom canoeing?' He put the papers down and looked right at her. 'Miss Wood,' he sighed. 'Is anybody in your family in medicine?'

Fiona swallowed. She couldn't think of anyone. She was from a mining village in Yorkshire, for goodness sake. Then it hit her. Of course.

'My brother.'

'Your brother?' said the dean. 'And what's his name?'

Before she could answer, the professor leaned across to the dean. 'This is David's sister,' he murmured. 'Did you see the try on Saturday?'

The dean's eyes widened.

'On the back page of the *Sunday Telegraph*. And against the Welsh, too. Couldn't be better.'

The dean looked at Fiona again. 'And you say David Wood is your brother?'

At once the mood shifted. The whole conversation turned to Saturday's rugby. David was playing for Saracens, one of London's big clubs. He'd previously played for St Thomas's, been captain of the United London Hospitals; he'd even trialled for England's Under 23s.

On the weekend, Saracens had played Pontypool. The Welsh front row were like giants, built like a stack of bricks. David was tall enough, six foot four, but he was slim. Compared to the Pontypool lads, he looked like Bambi.

Fiona could still see Sunday's headline:

WOOD CRASHES OVER THE TRY LINE DRAPED IN WELSHMEN

David's try had won Saturday's game. He was a hero.

The three of them chatted rugby a while longer, then the dean turned to the professor. The professor nodded. Fiona's heart stopped beating quite so hard.

'It's been a pleasure, Fiona,' the dean said.

As they showed her out of the interview room, they spotted David waiting for Fiona in the echoing hallway. He stepped forward as they approached.

'Don't worry,' the dean nodded to David. 'She should be fine.'

And not many months later, Fiona was headed to London. She was in!

8

Last (wo)man standing

The smell hit Fiona first. Formalin and chemicals, clawing at the back of her throat. Grabbing at her eyes, her nose. It was 1975, her first day at St Thomas's Medical School, and their first class was dissection.

The dissection room was huge, with high windows, bare walls and a floor that echoed every sound. Long stainless-steel tables were distributed around the mopped floor, shrouded in white sheets.

Under the sheets lay, what? Human bodies? Fiona swallowed back the bitter chemical taste, and her fear with it.

What if she'd made the wrong decision, applying to Tommy's? There'd be no nasty smells in physics. No chemicals in maths. What if she didn't like it?

'What stinks?' complained a dark-haired boy. 'Gross!'

A few others joked and jostled nervously, holding their noses.

Busting with anticipation, Fiona blinked back the pain in her eyes and tried to focus. She counted in her head. Twelve. She was one of just twelve girls in her year. The other 60-plus students were boys. No problem. Why should it matter if she was a boy or a girl?

The professor walked into the room with a swish of his white coat.

'Today you will begin to know your way around the inside of the human body,' he announced, pinning each of them with his steady gaze. 'Remember. The cadavers under these sheets were once people. Those people donated their bodies to the hospital so that you may learn the secrets of the human form …

And how to heal it.'

The professor's eyes roved the room.

'You are to treat cadavers with respect at all times. It is a privilege to work with these bodies, not a right.' He fell silent then. Fiona shivered, suddenly aware of how cold it was in here.

Cadavers in teaching

For hundreds of years, medical students have learned basic human anatomy by dissecting dead bodies, called cadavers. Today, these bodies are gifted by people who want to donate their body when they die.

Then, without warning, the professor folded back a sheet, revealing...

Well, Fiona couldn't tell. She was too short to see.

Thankfully, several of the boys stepped backwards almost at once. Good. Fiona wriggled into place.

An arm. He had revealed a pale brown human arm. Still attached to its body, judging from the shapes beneath the rest of the sheet.

Fiona watched closely as the professor showed them the correct way to attach a fresh scalpel blade, gripping it with forceps then sliding it down onto the handle.

'Cadavers do not bleed,' he announced. 'If you see blood, it will be your own.'

A couple more students stepped backwards from the table. Fiona hardly noticed as the dark-haired boy left the room.

She leaned in. Watched as the professor explained how hard to push, how deep to cut.

Pale yellow fat. Ivory tendons. The rust of embalmed flesh.

The bright white of bone, shining through stretched muscles.

It was incredible, Fiona couldn't look away. She didn't notice other students leaving the room. She didn't feel the cold, wasn't bothered by the formalin fumes.

She watched as the professor moved one of the fingers on the dead hand and saw how the tendons and muscles worked together so perfectly. How exquisite this thing was, the human body. So much detail, so much beauty.

This, then, was medicine, Fiona marvelled – this sort of magic and exploration and elegance. How could it be that all these things worked together to somehow support life? It was phenomenal. Could she one day do this? Not to a dead body, but to a living, breathing person?

If this is what a surgeon does, Fiona thought, fiercely, then this is what I will be.

She'd been at medical school less than a day, but already she knew. The beauty of it overwhelmed her. Here was a way she could contribute. Here was a way she could be useful in the world.

When she told her friends that she wanted to be a surgeon, many of them squirmed. Especially the ones who had fainted in that first dissection.

'You want to chop people up?' they said, faces screwed up. 'How can you enjoy that?'

Even Fiona realised it was a little strange. What kind of person enjoyed repairing someone on an operating table with a scalpel and some stitches? A surgeon, she thought. And that's the sort of person I want to be.

Many others – staff and students alike – laughed at Fiona. 'Girls can't be surgeons,' they'd remind her. 'Best decide on something else.'

'Being a surgeon is no job for a woman,' another would say.

'Only the very best med graduates get to study surgery. Surgery is no place for a girl.'

Fiona's blood boiled, but she couldn't fight back with her fists this time. And there was no point in arguing. Talk was just talk. She forced herself to stay calm. Don't waste an ounce of your energy on empty words, she decided. Just get to work, show them what you can do.

Instead of fighting, Fiona developed a new way to deal with her bullies. If anyone told her girls couldn't be surgeons, she'd just give them an innocent smile, making her eyes go all wide and doe-like.

'But I'm really good at needlework and embroidery,' she'd say. 'Does that help?' Then she'd walk on by. There's no point wasting my time, she thought. There's only one sure way I can change their minds...

Mum and Dad agreed. They often came down from Yorkshire to visit, bringing with them positive words, loads of hugs and fresh vegetables from the garden. 'Remember,' said Mum. 'Grasp this nettle and don't let go.'

It was Mum who'd sorted a place for Fiona at Ackworth School, and it was David who'd helped Fiona across the line to earn her spot at Tommy's. Now, the nettle was in Fiona's hand. Hanging on to it was all up to her.

Fiona poured herself into her studies. Worked as hard as she could. But the same professors who were so energetically telling her that girls could never become surgeons were also the ones who would decide if she'd be allowed to study surgery. What chance did she have?

One afternoon, she walked the galleries of the Hunterian Museum, trying to think. The Hunterian was a medical museum, filled with skeletons, dissected body parts and strange surgical instruments from hundreds of years ago. There weren't any dinosaurs, but there may as well have been.

They'll be looking for any chance to turn you away, she thought. You're going to need to be better than all the other students. If you want to study surgery, you're going to need to be so outstanding, they can't possibly turn you away.

So, she worked harder than ever, grasping every opportunity that came her way. She organised a trip to India to study malnutrition in pregnancy. She travelled to Kenya and Tanzania in Africa to collect fossils as part of her anthropology class. She even wrote her first research paper, and with all her fingers and toes crossed, submitted it to the British Journal of Nutrition. It was rejected.

The Leakey camp
In Tanzania, Fiona worked at the Leakey camp, made famous by archaeologists Dr Louis Leakey and Dr Mary Leakey. The Leakeys led decades of research at the Olduvai Gorge site, which contained bones and tools belonging to our early human ancestors. In 1959, Mary discovered a 1.75-million-year-old skull belonging to a hominid, nicknamed Nutcracker Man for its huge teeth.

Fiona was disappointed, but she didn't give up, and eventually, her dedication paid off. She was granted permission to take the surgery course.

That night was a celebration. Fiona was one step closer to becoming a surgeon! She knew the road ahead would be hard, but she could never have imagined where it would lead, or how she'd find the courage to keep walking.

9

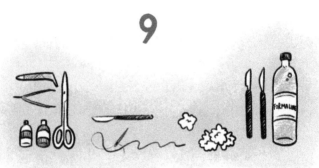

Part-time morgue

Surgical school was harder – and more exciting – than Fiona ever imagined. She had classes in general surgery, orthopaedics, paediatrics, eye surgeries, gut surgeries, heart surgeries…

And although she enjoyed it all, there was one class that really captured her imagination.

Plastic surgery.

A plastic surgeon's job was to help, Fiona quickly realised. They helped people who'd had accidents, they rebuilt injured hands, damaged limbs, disfigured faces. They helped people with deformities, babies born with cleft palates, people burned by fire or scalded by hot water. Here, Fiona thought, was an opportunity to do some real good. One operation could have a tangible, long-lasting impact on an injured person's life.

Cleft lip and cleft palate result when a baby's mouth has not finished developing by the time it is born. The baby might have a split or opening in their upper lip and gum area through to the roof of their mouth. Cleft palates and lips can be corrected with plastic surgery.

She watched as her teachers performed early microsurgeries. She saw surgeons use microscopes with robotic hinged arms to sew together blood vessels that were as thin as spaghetti. Every knot in every stitch had to be perfect, had to stay tied against the pulsing of blood and the pumping of oxygen.

It seemed to Fiona that plastic surgeons had to use their imaginations, too. They had to dream of ways to make a patient's life better. And plastic surgery seemed to go hand in hand with research and innovation. These surgeons worked right at the cutting edge of what was newly possible, and what was possible seemed to keep changing and growing and expanding. Fiona experienced it all, soaked it all in.

She found she could focus entirely on the moment, as soon as the doors to an operating theatre closed. All that existed of the world was the injured person on the operating table. Everything in that instant was about keeping that person alive.

How much trust people place in their surgeon, she thought. How vulnerable someone is when they're asleep. Asleep when I pick up my knife. Asleep when I sew them back together. She found it hard to believe that someone could give her permission to cut their body. They allow me to inflict pain because they trust I can help, she realised. I must never, ever take that trust for granted.

Fiona developed a habit of giving her best to every moment. Every time she walked into an operating theatre, into a hospital ward, she'd give her patients 100 per cent of her focus. Because that's what they deserve, she realised. I need to make each and every person feel I am there for them.

Of course, not everyone gave her that same respect.

'Isn't there a proper doctor who can help?' some patients would ask. 'A man doctor?'

'What are you still doing here?' some fellow students would jeer.

'Do you see any other girls doing surgery?'

The old Fiona would've put up her fists. The new Fiona didn't waste her time. 'Surgery is tricky, but I'm such an accomplished seamstress,' she'd say. 'Haven't you seen my gorgeous needlework?'

But beneath all her jokes, she was feeling worn down. All this negativity was like a black hole. She needed to make sure it didn't suck away her energy. She needed a way to stay positive. So, for every person who was negative, Fiona decided to find many more people who were positive. She remembered the way people had treated her big brother, Geoff. They'd never dreamed Geoff would get into Cambridge, they sneered when he said he'd study law. Well, now he was a lawyer. With a degree from Cambridge University. Anything was possible.

What we all need, Fiona decided, is more positivity in life. People who'll support us instead of knocking us down.

One of those people was Fiona's teacher, a plastic surgeon himself, who had admired Fiona's surgical skills.

'How do you feel about taking on a bit of extra research work?' he asked.

Soon Fiona found herself absorbed in yet another calling: the pursuit of answers and the discovery of new things.

Fiona's job was to learn more about human blood vessels, how they worked, how they might be used in new ways to put the human body back together, plastic-surgeon style.

To do this, she had to spend day after day working on cadavers. And that meant working in the morgue.

The morgue was deep beneath the hospital, where dead bodies were stored. It was a cold dark place when the lights were off. But who worked with the lights off?

Fiona didn't find the morgue spooky. But it was chilly, and she quickly learned to choose thick socks. Now, she slid her blade down the centre of the cadaver's chest, right from that little hollow at the base of the throat down to the bottom of the ribs.

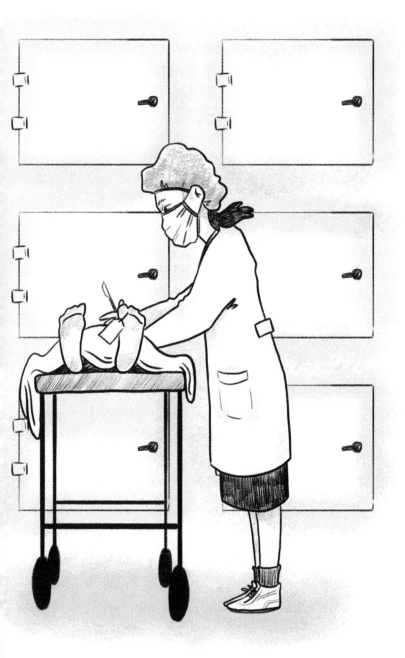

Through her gloves she couldn't feel the skin, but it looked soft and cold as it slid apart, revealing the yellow of fat, the dark red of muscle. She reached her fingertips under the muscle, between the bone, and pulled…

In moments like this, she was completely absorbed. Captivated. Here she was, working as a dissection dogsbody in the morgue, and it was fascinating. Learning about the human body, gathering knowledge, practising the skills and critical thinking that would help her become an even better surgeon.

Fiona worked hard, turned up day after day, used every opportunity as a chance to show what she could do. Slowly, people stopped commenting on her skirt or her hair and began to see her work.

Because after all, thought Fiona, as she inserted her knife once again, we're all the same on the inside.

Then, disappointment struck. Fiona failed her general surgery fellowship examination for the Royal College of Surgeons in London. It was a tough exam to pass, everyone knew it. Many students had to do the exam four or five times.

But Fiona had studied hard and was as ready as she thought she could be.

'I just got unlucky,' she explained to Dad later that week.

Dad only shrugged. 'The harder you work, the luckier you get.'

Ouch! But it was just the kick in the pants she needed. She studied harder and passed the exam on her very next try, qualifying as a surgeon in both London and Edinburgh in 1985.

Ten years had passed since Fiona's first dissection class at Tommy's, when she'd fallen in love with surgery. And along the way, she'd also fallen in love with Tony Kierath, a particularly smart fellow student. Tony was an Australian with a love of sport and an accent to die for. What followed was a whirlwind romance that swept Fiona off her feet.

'Y'know, if you marry me, you'll have to move to Australia,' Tony joked one day, but she could see in his eyes he was serious.

'Alright,' she said. 'It's a deal.' Because what could be better than living on a beach with Tony!

They were married their first free weekend.

Fiona soon scored a job at the super-respected East Grinstead Burns Unit of Queen Victoria Hospital, London. Here, an innovative plastic surgeon from New Zealand, Dr Archibald McIndoe, was doing mind-blowing things to help burns patients.

At one point, a little boy of four years came into the clinic. He'd been burned by spilled coffee when he was only two, and as he showed Fiona his scars, her heart stopped. She and Tony had a child of their own by now. She couldn't imagine her little Tom suffering what this boy was suffering. His scars were painful and deforming, and as he grew, the scarred skin couldn't grow with him, so it twisted and tore at his body.

I've got to be able to do better than this, Fiona thought, blinking back her tears. I have to work out how to make things better.

10

G'day,
Fiona

By 1987, Fiona and Tony had decided it was time for a change. From her window seat in the plane, Fiona stared and stared. This – this wide, brown, flat country, with its long stretches of blue beach – was her new home.

'We're going to live near the ocean,' she declared, and Tony laughed. She grinned at her husband. 'What? I'm serious.'

Tony didn't doubt it for a moment. Once Fiona set her mind to something…

By five the next morning, she was out and about with Tom and new baby Jess, exploring their new home. By Sunday, they'd borrowed Tony's sister's car and were driving up and down the coast, searching for a home that might fit their budget – and their growing family.

'This!'

As soon as she saw it, Fiona knew. It was a small house, but big enough for more kids if they wanted. And best of all, it was in City Beach.

'Even the name has "beach" in it,' she said happily.

Fiona couldn't believe her luck. Perth was glorious. After only three days they'd had more sunshine than Yorkshire had in a year.

'Does it ever rain?' she asked.

Tony grinned. 'Maybe in a month or two.'

Fiona made a habit of her 5 a.m. wakeup call – it was the perfect time to walk on the beach – and she had wasted no time in applying for jobs. But…

'I'm sorry,' said the man in the hospital administrative office. 'It's clear that you're enthusiastic, which is commendable, it's just…'

'Just what, doctor?' she asked.

He held out his hands – long, surgeon's hands – as if to apologise. 'Your children.'

Fiona waited. What about her children? She had two kids and hadn't hidden the fact. Did men have to hide their children to get a job?

She waited for the doctor to explain, letting the silence stretch until it went from awkward to uncomfortable and on, to excruciating. Eventually, he felt compelled to speak.

'It's just … you have children. You won't be able to do the job.'

Fiona bit back the anger that instantly flared. This was a job she desperately wanted. At a respected hospital. Just down the road from her new home. There was no way she'd let someone else's idea of what she could and couldn't do take this chance away.

She sat straight in her chair, looked the man in the eye. 'Doctor,' she said calmly. 'The only way we'll find out whether or not I can do the job is if you give me the job.'

Then she waited.

He waited, too.

Give me a chance, she thought fiercely. Just give me a chance.

Finally, Fiona walked out of that office with a job, but not the job she wanted. She'd been given a position as a general surgeon, not a plastic surgeon.

And just because one doctor had offered her a job, didn't mean she'd won over all the others.

Many of her new colleagues were supportive, but some were still wary of accepting a woman into their midst.

But gradually, week by week, Fiona began to prove that she had what it took. In 1989 she started as a trainee plastic surgeon at Sir Charles Gairdner Hospital, where she became close friends with Harold McComb, a Founding Member of the Australian Society of Plastic Surgeons. Like Fiona, Professor McComb was focused on making things better.

'Today doesn't have to be *criticised*,' he was fond of saying, 'but it should be *analysed*. One should never think that today is as good as it gets.'

Anytime she forgot this, Fiona just looked at the photo she kept beside her desk. It was a picture of the little boy from London, the boy who'd been scarred by the cup of coffee.

By now it was well known that fast action was vital for burns victims. The skin is the body's protective barrier. When layers of skin are burned, the body can't regulate its own temperature, it can't retain fluids, and it can't protect itself from infections. The faster a burn can heal, the faster the skin's protective barrier can be restored.

But some burns took forever to heal…

In 1990, a patient was admitted to Royal Perth Hospital with devastating burns. Fiona still wasn't qualified as a plastic surgeon, but she and her fellow trainees were touring the Royal Perth wards as part of their teaching rounds. When they saw this patient, it was clear she was dying. Her burns wouldn't heal; her body was fighting multiple infections. The doctors had tried all sorts of things to heal her, but nothing was working.

Then, driving home from the hospital one day, Fiona was listening to the radio. She heard something that sprouted into an idea: At Monash University, a scientist and a surgeon had just returned from Boston in the USA, where researchers were growing sheets of skin in laboratories. Incredibly, they could personalise skin, growing a small sample of a patient's own skin into more skin.

What if this new skin could be used to treat burns? Maybe the Royal Perth patient's injuries would finally heal…

Desperately, Fiona picked up the phone. 'Could it work?' she asked the burns team at Monash University, John Masterton and Joanne Paddle. 'Might it be possible?'

'It's certainly worth a try,' they agreed.

Fiona contacted the doctor in charge of the dying patient. 'Do you think we might try growing sheets of new skin?'

He also answered, 'It's worth a try.'

Next, Fiona contacted the administrator of Royal Perth Hospital. 'Mr Beresford,' she began, 'you don't know me, and I don't really work at your hospital, but there's a patient whose life I think we can save.'

She outlined her plan: harvest some of the patient's skin, then send it to Monash to be grown into sheets. 'If we treat her with her own skin, that could be her best chance.'

Beresford agreed. 'If you can find the money, you can do it.'

Fiona's next call was to the CEO of Ansett Airlines, Reg Ansett. 'Do you have an appointment?' his secretary asked.

'No,' Fiona replied. 'But I'm a doctor.'

That seemed to work. Soon she was telling her story again.

'I'm Dr Wood and you don't know me, but we have a patient who is dying. I think she might survive if you can help send a specimen to Melbourne, just a specimen, it won't take up a seat.'

Fiona held her breath. What would Reg say? Would he fly the skin specimen for free?

To her delight, Reg said yes.

Back at Royal Perth Hospital, Fiona carefully harvested a sample of the patient's unburned skin – a piece about the size of a twenty-cent coin. She packaged this skin into a sterile container and had it flown urgently to Monash University. There, under germ-free conditions and in a world-class medical laboratory, cells from the patient's skin were encouraged to grow and multiply. In thirty days, they had grown into sheet after sheet of healthy skin.

When Ansett Airlines flew the skin sheets back to Perth, they paid for John Masterton and

Ansett Airlines was one of Australia's major domestic and international airlines until 2001.

Joanne Paddle to fly over, too. Under the bright lights of Royal Perth Hospital's germ-free bone marrow laboratory, they worked with Fiona to carefully apply the fragile sheets of skin onto the patient's wounds. Fiona kept her hands steady and her face calm, but all the while, a little voice was echoing in her head. Was this the right thing? What if it didn't work?

But another, louder voice fought back. There is no other way. If you don't try this new approach, she will certainly die.

In just days, Fiona had her answer. The surgery was a success! Healthy skin began to grow back, healing the burns in just three weeks.

But then, weeks later, tragedy struck. A fungal infection had found its way into the patient's heart and it wasn't possible to resuscitate her. The patient couldn't be saved.

That night, driving home down Chancellor Parade, Fiona forced back her tears. This is not about you, she told herself. You can't just sit back and cry. That's not going to help anybody. She thought of Harold McComb, how he was always trying to make tomorrow better.

What can you learn from this tragedy? she demanded of herself. How can you take something from this that will make the future better?

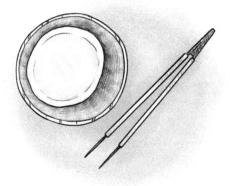

11

We're not perfect

Fiona continued to push herself. She wanted to learn more, reach further, do the very best that she could, every time. In 1991 she qualified as a consultant plastic surgeon, 16 busy years after starting medical school. That same month, she was appointed the Director of the WA Burns Service and began full-time work at Royal Perth Hospital.

Then, in 1992, she was called upon to treat another badly burned patient.

It was the October school holidays. A 29-year-old dad had been helping a mate with some roofing work when petrol leaked into their generator. The generator exploded. The patient was admitted to Royal Perth Hospital with petrol burns to 90 per cent of his body.

Fiona knew his chances of surviving were almost zero. But if there's a chance, she thought, I'll give it everything I have.

Maybe growing his skin in the lab would also be his chance to survive?

He's young, Fiona told herself. He's fit. If anybody can survive this, he can.

She and her team set to work. They harvested a tiny sample of the patient's healthy skin and sent it to Melbourne. Then, as they waited weeks for his skin to grow, they fought to keep him alive.

Finally, an urgent package arrived.

Fiona treated the patient as best she could. Everything she'd learned from treating her first patient helped, but over and again she thought he would die. For weeks and months, he fought through incredible pain and wave after wave of infection.

This is it, Fiona thought. He won't bounce back now.

But he always did.

Night after night, Fiona would drive home from the hospital, exhausted and frightened for his life, driven by his courage. And drained from watching it all go wrong.

The patient's burns were healing, but at a price. The scars they left were creating their own problems. Paralysis. Pain. Ongoing surgeries and health issues that would continue for the rest of his life.

Many nights, after a long shift at the hospital, Fiona would call her mum and dad, just to hear the sound of their voices. They were still living near the gates to Ackworth School, but the eight-hour time difference between Perth and England melted away once they got chatting. They talked about the kids and work and friends, everything really. Whatever Fiona faced, and even though she'd moved to the other side of the world, she felt as if her parents were beside her, every step of the way.

After nine long months in hospital, Fiona's patient was finally discharged. His life had been saved, but it had also been changed forever. Fiona had called in every favour, used the latest and best of every available technology, but the

patient would still endure burns-related health challenges for the rest of his life. Was that good enough? Fiona asked herself. How could that ever be good enough? She couldn't stop turning it over in her head. Was this the best we could've done? Is this outcome the best he could've hoped for?

Soon, Fiona couldn't sleep. She was a mess, emotionally wrung out and exhausted. How could she cope, going forward? How could she ever go back to the operating table, knowing her patients would go through such terrible suffering, only to face ongoing lifelong challenges?

There were no easy answers.

She needed to get away, have a break from it all. She and Tony decided to pack up the kids and go camping. They spent the next few days pitching tents and pumping airbeds and soaking in the calm and chaos of a family camping holiday. Fiona and Tony and the kids played cards and went hiking and argued about who ate all the chocolate and why did Tom take my pillow, and Fiona realised: we're not perfect, and we never will be.

All I can do is my best, she decided, and my best will never be good enough. Because until the day

I can offer my patients scar-less healing, I must always strive to be better.

She returned to the hospital more determined than ever to make a difference. 'Every patient is an opportunity to learn,' she told her team. 'And the hard lessons are the ones that help us improve.'

'How can you do that?' a doctor asked. 'How can you see tragedy as an opportunity?'

'Because it's more useful than seeing only tragedy,' she answered.

Fiona started researching skin and scarring at night, borrowing space in a nearby medical laboratory. While the rest of the world was asleep, she focused on ways to grow skin more quickly.

'Even if it takes three weeks, there's still a 74 per cent chance of scarring,' Fiona said, chatting to researcher Marie Stoner, who was working in the same lab. 'Burns patients can't afford to wait,' she explained. 'The faster we can close their wounds, the better their chances.'

And one thing kept bugging Fiona. Skin sheets are grafted on, but grafting works best when there are blood vessels.

And there are no blood vessels in sheets of lab-grown skin.

So, there had to be a better, faster way. Right?

She continued working nights at the lab, searching for answers. Marie was soon captivated by Fiona's passion. They decided to work together.

'We need to grow a sheet of skin in just ten days if it's going to be much use,' Fiona told Marie, and the challenge was born. The pair applied for and won a grant from Telethon to fund their research.

They started by checking out the literature, scouring libraries, hunting through journals and chasing up researchers over the phone. Loads of other scientists were growing skin sheets. How were they doing it?

The literature is scientific shorthand for the massive body of research papers and trial results that exists across the scientific world. Any time a scientific paper is published, it is added to this global pool of knowledge in case someone else might find it useful. Reading and learning from the literature helps scientists from all disciplines improve on existing work.

'Why did you include this step?' Fiona would ask. 'Did you try any other ways?'

At this time, Fiona and Marie didn't invent anything new. They just cherry-picked the fastest steps, put it all together into a skin-culture dream-team methodology, and gave it a shot.

'Ten days!' reported Marie. 'Look! We can grow skin sheets in just ten days!'

'Fantastic!' cheered Fiona. 'Now, how can we grow it even faster?'

Over and again, the pair challenged each other to imagine new ways to harness the skin's own ability to regenerate.

'What if we could help the enzymes penetrate more quickly?'

'What if we use a split skin graft, instead of a full-width graft?'

They conducted experiment after experiment, celebrating each minute that they shaved off the time.

One morning, after a late night at the lab, Fiona walked into her family breakfast just in time to see her six-year-old tip a mug of coffee all down himself.

No!!!

'Out of the way!' she yelled, bundling her son into her arms and racing him to the shower. She knew that cooling any burn under a cold tap was the best first aid. Just twenty minutes of cool running water could reduce a burn by 80 per cent.

She pushed her son under the cold tap. He howled and howled.

'What on earth are you doing?' her husband asked, incredulous.

'Twenty minutes of running cold water,' she said. But surely Tony knew that?

Her son was still screaming. The burn must be bad.

'But it was cold,' Tony said.

'Excuse me?' Fiona turned off the tap. Her child stopped screaming, scrambled from the cold shower and grabbed a towel, lips shivering.

'The kettle hasn't even been on this morning,' Tony said. 'That was cold coffee, leftover from yesterday.'

Fiona sank to the floor with relief. And her six-year-old asked for another shower, warm, this time, to defrost.

12

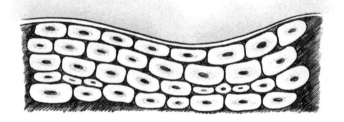

Italian mouth freshener

'Sorry, Fiona,' Marie said. 'This batch didn't seem to grow all the way.'

The sheet of skin Marie held up looked as if moths had been eating it. It was shabby, full of holes. But Fiona's patient needed skin and she needed it fast. There wasn't time for the sheets to grow all the way.

So, Fiona treated her patient using the holey half-grown skin.

A week later, she noticed something odd. Where she had used the holey sheets – ones that hadn't had time to grow all the way – her patient's wounds healed faster.

It happened the same way in her next patient. 'Huh,' she thought. 'I wonder…'

Cell differentiation
Every living thing begins as a bunch of cells. As you grow and develop, your cells divide and specialise (differentiate) into different types of cells: heart cells, nerve cells, blood cells, skin cells and more.

Fiona and Marie turned their attention to the biology of skin culture. Each skin sheet grew from a broth of cells, all floating about in suspension, like a cell soup. So what caused these cells to divide? What made them change into the specialist cells that make up healthy skin? How could they use this knowledge to help burns patients?

They discovered that patients' cells were growing fastest after just three or four days, when they were still at the soup stage.

'What if we could introduce a patient's own growing cells at just the right time …?'

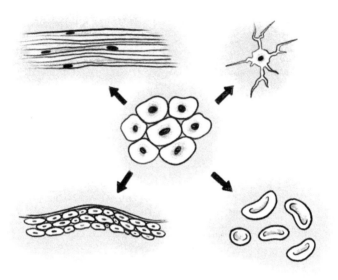

The idea was born. Fiona and Marie began to harvest the growing cells earlier and earlier, while they were still floating in the cell soup.

But how do you apply soup to a wound?

'Maybe we could trap it under a plastic dressing?'

'Maybe make a sort of blister of cells?'

Marie and Fiona threw ideas around, going back and forth with wilder and more imaginative solutions until at last, inspiration struck.

'What if we just spray them on?'

'You mean like spray-paint skin?'

'Sure, I mean, why not?'

The pair raced to Fiona's car. Their first stop: the art shop. Their second? The chemist. They bought every kind of spray-on aerosol gizmo and gadget they could find. If there was a way to spray on skin cells, they were determined to find it.

They tried the nozzles on just about everything that sprayed. Deodorants. Spray paints. Cooking oils. Air fresheners. Disinfectants. Nose sprays. Throat sprays. Until at last...

'Success!' Marie cried. 'Look at these results!'

The nozzle on a bottle of Italian mouth freshener was just right. It fit tightly onto a standard 5 ml syringe. Using it allowed them to deliver more active cells than ever before. But this was only the start of the journey...

'What if we didn't need to send skin samples away to a lab?' Fiona mused.

Now that really was impossible. Where else could you grow cells, if not in a lab?

'But healthy bodies make their own skin all the time, right?' Marie reasoned. 'A healthy body is basically its own tissue culture flask.'

But burns patients were so sick, their body could no longer regenerate skin.

So what if…?

'Could the best place to grow a patient's own cells be right on their wound?'

Fiona and Marie stared at each other from across the table. They began sketching, dreaming up a portable kit they could take into the operating room to harvest and then grow the patient's skin cells. For a long while, neither of them spoke. It was such an audacious idea. Then, they picked up their phones and began to dial.

They contacted experts in electronics, in cell culture, in plastic moulding, and they asked for help.

The result, after all their years of imagination, collaboration and work, was a totally self-contained portable skin culture kit. The kit meant that surgeons could grow a sample of a patient's skin right there in the operating theatre. The whole process of getting the skin cells ready took just thirty minutes.

'You can harvest the skin cells you need to cover the wound while you're in surgery, prepping the wound,' Fiona explained. 'Then it's as simple as spraying it on.'

It was 1993. Fiona began using the kit to treat patients straight away. The results were immediate.

'But you haven't done a clinical trial!' critics said. 'What you're talking about has never been done before. It's unscientific to treat people without first doing a proper double-blind trial.'

> **Clinical trials** are used to test a new medical treatment or to compare a new treatment with an existing treatment.

So, Fiona and her team embarked on trials, using spray-on skin cells from healthy donor sites to heal damaged skin sites. They also trialled the technology on different types of burns, building know-how as they worked.

What they found was electrifying. Thanks to spray-on skin, they were able to perform surgeries sooner and there was less need for painful skin grafts. Patients healed faster, too, and their risk of scarring was significantly reduced.

Children, especially, healed faster and better than ever before. Today, 80 per cent of children who are admitted to the Royal Perth Hospital children's burns unit will have no visible scarring as they grow.

By 1995 Fiona was using spray-on skin routinely, and in 1999, she and Marie established the

McComb Foundation, named after Fiona's mentor and friend, Harold McComb. The aim of the foundation? To raise money for researching new and better ways to treat burns.

Thanks to the foundation's success, in 2000, Fiona and Marie were able to found a company to commercialise their research. They called it Clinical Cell Culture (C3, now Avita Medical) and set up in Technology Park, Bentley, Western Australia.

At first, Fiona wasn't comfortable with the idea of *selling* these life-saving technologies. She'd devoted her career to working in the public service, to helping people regardless of who they were or how rich they might be.

But she knew money was important. More money would allow more research, and more research would mean better outcomes for many thousands of patients. And Fiona had learned that just *discovering* something wasn't enough. Other hospitals were still not using spray-on skin, but she wanted patients everywhere to benefit from surgeons using it.

One of her first investors was Australian Olympic basketballer Luc Longley. As he walked into her office, all 218 centimetres of him, Fiona grinned.

This is about as close as I'll come to the Olympics, she thought wryly. How much had changed since her childhood dream. Her 400-metre sprint had turned into a lifelong marathon.

Around this time, Fiona began working with Australian oil and gas company Woodside Petroleum to develop a disaster plan. Woodside operated an offshore gas production platform, called North Rankin A, one of the largest such platforms in the world. This thing was a giant, towering nearly 100 metres out of the ocean, secured to the ocean floor 125 metres below. It was large enough to house 120 people and produced 50,000 tonnes of gas every day.

If any disaster were to strike, North Rankin A was a long way from help being 1,500 kilometres from Perth to Karratha, and another 135 kilometres out to sea.

Woodside needed a disaster plan, and they had good reason for wanting to prepare: on 6 July 1998, hundreds of people were working onboard a similar offshore platform, named Piper Alpha, near Aberdeen, Scotland. The day had started well, but by ten o'clock that night, a missing safety valve led to a deadly mistake. Gas seeped out, causing an explosion that ripped through firewalls and pipes. The entire platform became a billowing fireball. Only 61 of the 226 people on Piper Alpha survived. Eleven of the survivors had serious burns.

The world was left in shock. Such a disaster could never be allowed to happen again. Safety regulations were tightened, disaster training was increased, and Woodside came to the Royal Perth burns team to work out the very best way to deal with a mass burns casualty crisis. If the worst were ever to strike again, how fast could they evacuate? How quickly could they get injured people to medical help? And what was the very best way of co-ordinating a response?

Together, Fiona and the Burns Service of WA team worked to develop a rigorous disaster plan. From flying in helicopters across oil rigs to teaching basic first aid, they simulated a disaster response, working to prepare everybody to be able to respond to a mass burns emergency. They called it Exercise Icarus and *'The right treatment in the right place at the right time'* was their motto.

In July 2002, Fiona's team sent their recommendations to the Australian Health Ministers' Advisory Council.

Fiona wrote: 'Fortunately, on an ordinary day or month, not many patients are burned. But on an extraordinary day, on a catastrophic day, we're going to need to respond on a much larger scale. And the way we can do that is by supporting each other, by working together, across the country.'

She went on to outline the best ways to achieve this, and by August, these recommendations were approved. Australia and New Zealand's Mass Casualty Burn Disaster Plan was in place, and there were congratulations all round.

No one had any idea that in less than two months' time, they'd be called upon to carry out the plan for real.

13

Mass casualty burn disaster

The week before the 2002 October school holidays, things were busy at the Burns Unit of Royal Perth Hospital. The unit was full. Fiona and her team were working hard and she was looking forward to a break. She had a friend's wedding coming up and was planning some time off with her family.

Many staff felt the same way. Senior registrar Vijith Vijayasekaran worked with Fiona in the burns unit till late on Friday afternoon. He and his wife, Priya, an anaesthetist, had booked a week's holiday on the island of Bali, Indonesia, and they were counting down the hours.

Vij and Priya flew out the next day, Saturday, October 12. They could never have imagined how their holiday would turn out.

That night, while Vij and Priya were relaxing in their hotel, the streets of Kuta, Bali, were full. Tourists and partygoers were crowding the bars and clubs, talking and laughing, enjoying the humid night air. There were Aussie football teams celebrating, friends reuniting, people pinching themselves at how lucky they were to be in such a beautiful part of the world.

Then, in an instant, everything changed.

At 11 p.m., a terrorist group detonated nearly 1,000 kilograms of explosives in a series of three bombs. The first bomb exploded inside the Sari Club, instantly killing nine people. Panicked and hurt, survivors rushed from the burning building and into the street. There, just seconds later, a second bomb detonated. Trees were flattened, buildings were reduced to rubble. Hundreds of people were injured, hit with shrapnel and debris and burned by the fires. Across town, a third bomb exploded outside the American Consulate in Denpasar.

Bali's emergency services swung into action. The wail of sirens split the warm night, queues of ambulances formed, and the local Sanglah Hospital was quickly overwhelmed by the hundreds of injured and traumatised people arriving at its doors.

But at eight o'clock on Sunday morning, as Fiona was walking on her beloved Perth beach, she had no idea of any of this. Her friends' wedding was that afternoon and she was thinking about which shoes she might wear. Then her phone rang. It was Anthony Williams, a doctor on duty at Royal Perth Hospital.

'Fiona,' he said, voice strained. 'Something's happened.'

Anthony had just got off the phone to Vij, who was speaking directly from the chaos and overcrowding of Sanglah Hospital. As soon as they'd heard about the disaster, Vij, Priya and several other Australian doctors already in Bali had raced to volunteer at the hospital. They knew their medical training and experience would be invaluable.

As quickly as he could, Anthony relayed all that Vij had told him.

Anthony's words charged at Fiona from down the phone, one after the other, over and over. She tried to absorb them, could only imagine the scene that staff at Sanglah Hospital were facing. The panic and pain, the helplessness of not having enough beds, enough operating theatres, enough time. You can't just bandage a burn and think everything's going to be okay. Burns victims often need months of treatment, of surgery, of rehabilitation. There was no way Bali's local hospitals could manage.

Vij was on the ground. He had burns training and he knew just how bad the situation was. Yet the number of people he was talking about, the sheer scale of it…

And in that moment, Fiona knew.

She willed herself to stay calm. This is exactly what you've been trained for, she told herself. This is what you've been dreading, and yet what you've been preparing for all these years.

She hung up from Anthony and dialled Bill Beresford, the executive director of Royal Perth Hospital. 'I think we have a problem,' she told him.

Then she dialled again, relaying the same message to Phil Montgomery, Director of Clinical Services.

'We're the closest major hospital,' she reminded them. 'They'll be evacuating patients here. I don't know how many, but a lot. At least double figures. If we're going to give these people the best care we can, we need to start preparing now.'

Almost immediately, the Mass Casualty Burn Disaster Plan they'd so carefully prepared only months ago was called into action.

All over Australia, burns experts cancelled their plans and booked their flights. At Royal Perth Hospital, Fiona met with the hospital's senior team to ensure the hospital would be ready. 'The Defence Force are helping evacuate. They're sending in the RAAF. The first plane should be in Bali by four o'clock. From there they're taking people to Darwin. We can expect our first patients at the crack of dawn Monday morning. Everything must be ready for then.'

The team knew how serious the situation was. 'We'll be ready,' they said. 'We'll be right where you need us to be.'

When everything was in place, there was nothing more anyone at Royal Perth could do. Except wait.

And try to get some rest. No one knew exactly what the next hours would bring.

A call came in from the Commonwealth Department of Health, in Canberra. 'It's vital you evacuate those patients from Bali as quickly as possible,' Fiona told them. 'The faster we can treat them, the—'

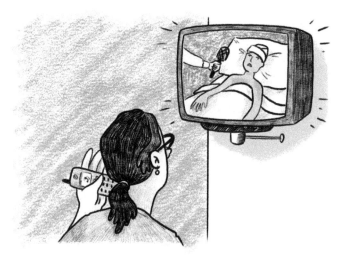

It was then that she saw the TV. At the back, high on the wall. Television crews were broadcasting from Kuta. Fiona's jaw dropped at the destruction; her heart sank at the chaos. Then the broadcast swapped, and Fiona had her first look inside Sanglah Hospital.

'Fiona?' said the voice at the other end of the line. 'Are you still there? Hello, Fiona?'

But Fiona couldn't speak. There, on the television, a reporter was interviewing Perth man, Peter Hughes. Peter was in a hospital bed, looking dazed, swollen, bandaged, but apparently quite calm. He was telling the reporter he was okay, that there were others worse off than him.

The need for speed

It is absolutely vital that burns victims receive urgent medical attention. Skin is your body's largest organ. It plays a crucial role in protecting you from infections, managing your fluid levels and maintaining your temperature. Without a healthy skin to do these jobs, burns victims are at risk of infections, dehydration and hypothermia. Faster treatment greatly improves patient outcomes and reduces the likelihood of physical scarring.

But one look and Fiona knew he was far from okay. This clarity, this strange lucid calm that Peter was showing despite his incredible injuries, it wasn't uncommon in people with serious burns. And she knew it wouldn't last.

Desperately, Fiona found her voice at last. 'Listen,' she spoke into the phone. 'We need to get these people out, or pretty soon they will be dead.'

The rest of Sunday passed in a blur. Fiona sent as many of her staff home as she could. 'Sleep,' she instructed. 'Eat. Because soon you may not have the chance.'

Fiona found herself entering a strangely calm place of focus. As the head of the burns unit, over the coming hours, days and months, tens of patients would be depending on her. Surgeons and staff would be looking to her to guide them. Many had never worked with her before. It was up to Fiona to form them into a team, to co-ordinate hospital beds and operating theatres and pain relief and medical care. And for how many patients? And how bad were their burns?

There was so much she didn't know. You're prepared, she told herself. You don't need to feel afraid. You have trained for this and you're surrounded by professionals who have trained for this. This is something we know how to do. You have it in your power to make a real difference. Find a way to move forward.

By early Monday morning, the mood in Royal Perth Hospital was tense. Outside, it was still cold and dark. Inside, everyone on the team was prepared and totally focused, waiting for their patients to arrive. Exercise Icarus had been a simulation. This would be the real thing.

Reports from Perth Airport began coming in around 2.30 a.m. Aeroplanes were arriving with evacuated people. An RAAF Hercules C-130. A Garuda flight. Even a private jet, on loan from media mogul Kerry Stokes.

Not long now.

The hospital had teams ready and waiting at the airport. Ambulances, paramedics and triage nurses in charge of quickly deciding where each patient needed to go. Walking wounded to Fremantle Hospital, or to Charles Gairdner Hospital, in Nedlands. Burns patients went straight to Royal Perth Hospital.

The wail of sirens filled the air. By 5 a.m. Monday morning, just 30 hours after the first explosion, twelve badly burned patients had been admitted to Royal Perth. More were expected.

A second triage team was set up in the emergency department at Royal Perth. Another sixteen critically ill patients arrived. Many were wheeled straight into surgery, for urgent, life-saving operations.

Others were sent to the Intensive Care Unit for help with breathing and support. Those who weren't urgent enough for surgery or ICU were moved to the burns unit.

ICU stands for Intensive Care Unit, a specialised hospital ward. ICUs are dedicated to seriously ill patients who require life support and close, round-the-clock care.

But their condition was still terribly urgent.

The job now was to act swiftly and courageously. To stabilise patients, manage their pain, protect them from infection. The team soon realised they wouldn't be dealing only with burns. The explosion had caused multiple other injuries: broken bones, shrapnel wounds, blast injuries, dehydration, shock and infection. There was so much to do, and it all needed to be done yesterday.

Royal Perth had already extended the burns unit into the neighbouring plastic surgery ward. All elective surgeries were cancelled, and the burns team had commandeered half of ICU, hoping against hope that there'd be enough beds. How could they turn anyone away?

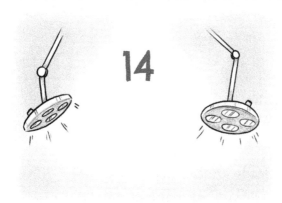

Round-the-clock teamwork

'We have four operating theatres, 19 surgeons, 130 medical staff,' Fiona announced, chairing a meeting in the hospital boardroom on Monday afternoon. She looked around the room at the surgeons and nurses who were looking to her for leadership.

'We have 28 badly burned patients,' she continued. 'More than we've ever had before. But we are a well-prepared team. And if more patients arrive, we won't turn anyone away. Not unless we can't do the job.'

In a usual week, Royal Perth Hospital might've seen three or four burns patients admitted. The Burns Unit might treat 20 serious burns patients in a year.

Already in the hours since their first patient had arrived, the team had thrown themselves into emergency surgeries, surgeries needed now, now, now, just to keep their patients alive.

Many of those patients were still being stabilised, but Fiona knew the hardest job was yet to come. Now they must work to heal as much of the damage as possible. Surgeries to seal wounds and restore function. But they had 28 patients, all urgently requiring round-the-clock attention and needing multiple, complicated surgeries, each many hours long...

'And that is the challenge,' Fiona told her team. 'We are absolutely required to do the very best job we can, the job we've been trained to do. It will be tough. But we're in a position to make a positive difference in the face of this disaster. To give each of these people the very best care we can, and there can be no better motivation than that. They each deserve the best personalised world-leading care that we pride ourselves on giving. And if we can't provide that, we need to work out why, and solve the problems.'

She looked around at the sea of faces.

Carmel McCormack, Director of Nursing at Royal Perth Hospital, stood up. 'We have three hours to make this happen,' she said. 'Let's meet back here then, and if we have any remaining problems, we'll sort them.'

The team moved out, each preparing for their own part in the journey to come. From storerooms to theatres, nursing to anaesthetics, ICU to physiotherapy. There could be no question of running out of supplies, no chance that an operating theatre would lie idle, no time when all the right experts weren't ready and waiting to do all the right things.

Fiona set up a whiteboard in the main office, a sort of mission control, and she used it to talk each surgical team through the challenges of their next surgery. Then she'd be back operating in her own theatre, or offering help to other teams.

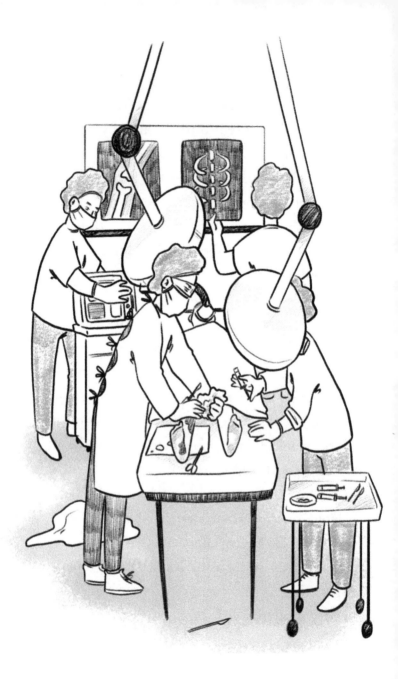

Everyone gave everything they had. Operating theatres stayed busy day after day, team after surgical team raced against time, rotating through shifts to stay fresh. Oxygen. Fluids. Wound cleaning. Infection control. Pain relief. Everyone pitched in, offered all that they had, worked side by side, doing everything possible to help their patients.

Surgical teams used every available method to treat the wounds, including skin grafts and donor skin and the newly invented spray-on skin. There were so many different burns, each complicated by shrapnel from the explosions, and bacteria from tropical Bali. Each patient received a different, personalised approach. Everyone worked to get the best results for their patients.

Hot operating theatres
Badly burned people can't regulate their own body temperature. To protect patients from becoming too cold, burns wards and surgical theatres are heated. A good first aid rule to remember is 'Cool the Burn, Warm the Patient'.

In these early days, Fiona's teams carried out thirty operations in a row. Some operations lasted more than ten hours. Most were complicated and required large teams, up to six nurses at a time. And all the while, the wards and operating theatres were warmed to a sweaty 32 degrees Celsius: burns victims need to be kept warm.

Slowly, the teams began to get to know their patients, people who'd come to Bali from New Zealand, England, Scotland and Germany. And then they'd come to Perth.

Almost immediately, patients' families and friends arrived from all over the world, along with cards, letters and flowers. Businesses and individuals sent donations of food, equipment, supplies. Thousands of ordinary Australians lined up to donate blood. The media also arrived. Soon, TV crews and newspapers were camped outside the hospital's doors. A window to Fiona's world had opened, and ordinary people saw for the first time what she was doing with spray-on skin.

Fiona and her team worked long, long hours, stopping only for sleep and meals, giving their all to the very best of their ability. But sometimes, even their very best wasn't enough.

Tragically, their first patient died within 72 hours. Twenty-nine-year-old Jodie O'Shea had saved up for her Bali holiday by working two jobs. But she had burns to 93 per cent of her body. Though the team worked hard to ease her pain, they couldn't save her life. Fiona bit back tears as she watched Jodie's mum Rhonda holding her daughter. Now isn't the time for you to cry, Fiona told herself. There are others who need your help.

One of those people was Connie Watson, a young triathlete who had arrived at Royal Perth with horrific burns and fractures. Fiona was at Connie's bedside when she came out of her coma.

'I know I'll never run again,' Connie said bravely, 'but will I be able to walk?'

Fiona looked her patient in the eye. 'You will walk again,' she said determinedly. 'You will run, you can even race again. You were a fit and healthy young woman. I have seen people like you survive injuries like this. I don't know if you are that person, but there is a chance for you. There is an opportunity for you to take your life back again and to live it how you want.'

The road ahead wouldn't be easy, Fiona knew it. But over many months, Connie worked through grief and pain and nine surgeries to regain her mobility. And even Fiona couldn't have predicted that Connie would one day race in the same

Ironman bike race as Fiona – in Busselton in 2008 – and beat her. As Fiona collapsed at the finish line, Connie was there to meet her. The two athletes – surgeon and patient – hugged each other tightly.

Other patients weren't as lucky.

Tracy Thomas had been admitted with terrible burns. Her three girls had arrived at the hospital to find their mum wrapped head-to-toe in bandages. Like many Bali patients, Tracy was battling multiple infections. Many of the infections were unique to Indonesia and resistant to antibiotics. Tracy's organs were shutting down and there was little the doctors could do.

Tracy's girls waited through three lengthy surgeries. They all hoped that each operation might give her another chance. But one week after the bombings, late on October 20, Tracy also passed away. She never woke from her coma, but her three daughters were there, at her bedside. Tracy was the second patient the team had lost, and the effect was devastating.

That night, when Fiona went home physically exhausted and emotionally spent, she found a surprise in her fridge.

Casseroles. Ready-to-heat meals, and lots of them.

Her friends had been cooking for her family, dropping meals off to Tony and the kids.

Fiona felt embarrassed. Her family weren't the ones suffering, they were healthy. They weren't the ones who needed help. Her immediate instinct was to push back.

'Thanks for thinking of us, Kel,' she told her friend, 'but my kids are fine, you don't need to worry. You don't need to send us any more food.'

Kel's reaction took Fiona by surprise. 'Why are you being so selfish?' she asked.

Selfish? Fiona had just spent most of a week working non-stop at the hospital. Selfish was the last word that she'd thought she might hear.

'We all want to help,' Kel went on. 'What's happened is so terrible, we all want a way to help. Making casseroles might not be as important as what you can do, but it's what I can do, and I need to do it. It's not weakness to ask for help, Fiona. We're all in this with you. We're all in it together.'

Fiona closed her eyes against the tears. Kel was right. Getting through every day was a team effort, and these last few days more than ever. People everywhere were doing extraordinary things to help each other through this tragedy, sending gifts, babysitting, volunteering for people they didn't even know. Kel was right. It wasn't weakness to accept help from others. Giving and accepting help were both vital.

And now, especially, Fiona needed to do both.

Just three weeks after the Bali bombing tragedy, 20 of Fiona's 28 patients were well enough to be discharged from Royal Perth Hospital and fly home to their local hospitals.

Peter Hughes, the man Fiona had first seen on TV at Sanglah Hospital, was admitted to Royal

Perth from Adelaide Hospital at this time, too. Soon, only Peter and three other Bali patients remained.

One was Simone Hanley, whose sister Renae had died in Bali on that awful night. Simone's mother, Maryjane, had flown from Sydney to keep vigil at Simone's bedside, but her daughter showed no sign of waking.

Simone had been severely injured, with burns to 75 per cent of her body. She was in an induced coma, wrapped in bandages, relying on a ventilator to breathe.

'Please save this one,' Maryjane begged Fiona.

But by December, the team knew the sand was sinking through their hands. After nearly two months of fighting wave after wave of infection, Simone was growing weaker. They tried everything, but on 9 December, 58 days after the bombing, Simone passed away.

Fiona and her team came close to crashing down.

But Fiona knew that for Simone's family, the pain must be infinitely worse.

She needed somewhere to let out all her grief. Somehow, she found herself in the hospital toilet and locked herself in there to weep. You need to get back out there, she told herself. You need to spend your precious energy helping, not weeping.

But how? How to find the courage to keep returning to the operating table, again and again?

She finally gathered herself, washed her face in the sink, and promised herself, right there and then, that she would honour these deaths. You will honour their suffering by doing everything you can to make things better, she told herself. You will focus on helping the people who will still need you.

Fiona and her team were able to save the lives of 25 of the 28 people who were evacuated to Royal Perth Hospital that terrible night. In all, 240 people were injured by the Bali bombings. Simone was the last of 88 Australians and 202 people to die as a result of the attack.

Eventually, by January 2003, 26-year-old Antony Svilisich was the only patient from the bombings still at Royal Perth. Antony had been burned across 64 per cent of his body. He'd been in a coma for 44 days before moving to the burns ward, where Fiona performed surgery after surgery to help heal his injuries.

When he was finally discharged from hospital, 86 days after the bombs, Fiona and her staff lined the hospital corridors to give him a standing ovation. Alongside them stood other Bali survivors, ex-patients who had returned to the hospital to wish Antony well.

Reporters queued up at the hospital door to interview him as he left.

'How does it feel, Mr Svilisich?' they asked.

'Words can't describe it,' he said. 'I've been looking forward to this day for a long time.'

With the last of her Bali patients discharged, Fiona thought her life would return to normal – or as normal as life can be for a burns surgeon.

How very wrong she was.

15

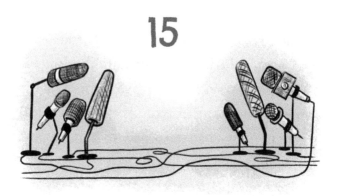

Australian
of the Year

Day after day, Fiona's inbox flooded with requests from the media. Television interviews. Guest segments. Panel discussions. Keynote speeches. The Bali bombings had opened a window into Fiona's world and the world wanted to know more.

Ordinary people learned for the first time of the life-changing work Fiona and Marie had been doing in burns research and spray-on skin. Doing so many interviews and appearances was exhausting, but after the bombings, Fiona realised how important it was to spread positivity wherever she could.

'We've lived through something extraordinary,' her colleague, paediatric surgeon Ian Gollow told her. 'Something we'll never have to see again, hopefully. But we've also seen people motivated for good in a way we've never seen before.'

Why does it take a tragedy to bring out the best in people? Fiona wondered. Why do we hide our human spirit? Our kindness, our respect, our integrity? Why don't we have the courage to share it all the time?

The more she and Ian talked, the more they realised: people are always out there, doing amazing things, all the time – it's just that we don't hear about it.

From that moment, Fiona began seeking out good news, stories about ordinary people doing extraordinary things, the sorts of stories that could bring hope. And she began shouting those stories to the rooftops.

'Enthusiasm breeds enthusiasm,' she'd tell anyone who would take notice. 'Why waste your energy on negative stories? Just imagine what we could achieve if we all gave our best all the time.'

Well, lots of people began to take notice.

In 2003, Fiona was awarded Member of the Order of Australia (AO) and later the Australian Medical Association's Contribution to Medicine Award. In 2005, she was voted Australia's most trusted person. She went on to win this accolade a massive six years in a row.

Also in 2005, Fiona and Marie won the Clunies Ross Award from the Australian Academy of Technological Sciences and Engineering, for their contribution to medical science in Australia. Fiona was over the moon. All these awards helped raise the profile of her work, attracting more funds and support for burns research and education.

Then there came another phone call, and once again, Fiona's life was changed forever.

'I've what?' she echoed into her phone.

'You've been nominated for Australian of the Year. Again.'

Fiona had been nominated the year before, when she'd won West Australian of the Year. Being nominated two years in a row was a huge achievement. But Fiona's response was the same as last time. Amazement.

Me? Australian of the Year? I'm not that sort of person. How could I justify people putting so much faith in me? How could I manage? If she won Australian of the Year, the prize would come with huge responsibilities.

Australian of the Year Awards
The Australian of the Year Awards can be won by any Australian of any age who has demonstrated outstanding achievement, contributions to the nation, and an ability to inspire fellow Australians. Do you know someone who fits the bill? Why not nominate them for this year's awards?

'You'll manage the only way you know how, Mum,' said her kids, smiling their congratulations. 'With lots of hard work!'

At the award ceremony in Canberra, Fiona tried to talk herself out of being nervous. There's no chance I'll win, she reasoned. The other nominees are so incredibly amazing.

Plus, the 2003 Australian of the Year had been Fiona Stanley, another West Australian medical professor. There was no way they'd go for two Fionas in a row. Right?

But then Prime Minister John Howard took the stage. 'And the winner of Australian of the Year for 2005 is … Fiona Wood,' he announced.

Jittery with nerves, Fiona somehow made her way to the front.

As she walked onto the stage, Warren Pearson, CEO of the Australia Day Council, leaned over. 'You *are* Australian, aren't you?' he joked.

'No,' she joked back, putting on her best Yorkshire accent. 'Does it matter?'

He went white.

'Just kidding,' she said quickly. 'Of course, I'm Australian. And I'm also proudly from Yorkshire.' Wow, she thought later. How lucky am I, to be able to honour my past and also strive for the future?

After her win, there was one question everyone wanted to ask: 'What is it you want to share with Australia?'

There was so much she wanted to say. In the end, she chose one thing:

'That every one of us is unique and special, every one of us has a gift, a gift we should share. If we don't, that gift is worthless … How often do we do less than our best? How often do we challenge those around us to be their best?'

As Australian of the Year, Fiona flew all over the country, giving speech after speech after speech. Around 600 talks in a single year! Pretty soon she'd added another skill to her bursting CV: she could fall asleep on an aeroplane, even before its wheels had left the runway.

One day I'll stand up and I won't know what to say, she sometimes thought, wondering at the privilege of having so many people interested in hearing her speak.

But she never slipped up.

Except, perhaps, just once. It was Sunday morning. Fiona was with her kids, wearing pink Ugg boots and a tracksuit at the ice-skating rink when her phone rang.

It was the organiser of a leadership conference at Curtin University. 'Ah, Dr Wood,' she began, 'Sir Charles Court is nearly finished…'

A sick feeling landed in Fiona's stomach. 'Right,' she said. 'So, that'll be my turn next…'

She had no time to do anything except ring some friends to collect her kids. When she gave an inspiring speech at Curtin University only minutes later, confessing her mistake, she was still sporting those gorgeous Uggies.

'And that's the first lesson of leadership in my house,' she told the crowd. 'If you don't get up early in the morning, you don't get the pink Ugg boots!'

That sure broke the ice, and the rest of the conference was a success.

Fiona found that people weren't only interested in her professional life. Over and again, she'd be asked the same question. 'How do you manage all this *and* six kids?'

Fiona never pretended it was easy, but she never hid the joy her family brought her either.

'Don't believe that if you want to be a surgeon you can't have children,' she'd often say, especially to young students. 'Choose your own path. Do what *you* want to do. And if someone tells you that you can't, just smile nicely and move on by.'

16

Fiona: into the future

Fiona is still chasing her dreams. Together with her team at the Fiona Wood Foundation, and researchers and scientists around the world, Fiona is dedicated to changing what is possible when it comes to healing burns. Thanks to her team's lifesaving and life-changing work, the time a burns victim needs to spend in hospital has been halved, and a massive 75 per cent of patients are able to achieve good quality of ordinary life after only six months.

Unfortunately, Fiona's work is never complete. Burns injuries continue in a constant stream. Bushfires, road accidents, camping accidents, scalds and mass casualty disasters, like plane crashes, volcanic eruptions or the Bali bombings, are always around the corner.

Since that dreadful night in 2002, Fiona's team has treated around 4,000 patients. Spray-on skin has been approved by the US Food and Drug Administration and similar organisations in many other countries. It is now being used to help many more thousands of people around the globe.

To treat and rehabilitate a badly burned person requires an extraordinary combination of science, technology and dedication. From highly trained experts to the incredibly high-tech wards and theatres they work in, from artificial skins and cellular frameworks to ground-breaking work with laser therapies to un-scar scars... Who could ever have imagined such life-saving leaps could be made in less than 30 years?

Well, we know at least one person imagined this future. Fiona has never lost her love of discovery, her motivation to understand more. She is still working hard to make our future futures even more astounding.

'What if we could print new skin with a 3D printer?' she asks. 'What if surgeons could operate with an intelligent knife, one that analyses human cells in real-time, one that gives you instant feed-back on which cells are burned and which are still alive? What if we could train the brain to change our body's capacity to heal? What if we could *think* ourselves whole?'

Fiona knows these might be wild dreams.

But dreams started all of it.

'And if you can't dream something,' she says, 'how can you ever achieve it?'

Right now, she's working on making those wild dreams come true. She's training the burns innovators of the future. She's working with businesses, patients and ordinary people to raise money for more research. And she's collaborating with scientists from across the globe – data analy-sists, engineers, nanotechnologists, neurophysio-logists, cardiologists, biochemists – to find new pieces of the puzzle that will solve the mystery of scar-less healing. Because by working together, by combining the skills and passions of multiple scientists, mathematicians and medical experts, we can achieve extraordinary things.

'I have seen the power of basic science at the bedside,' Fiona says. 'I have seen how it can make such a huge difference, how it can ease suffering. I have seen it in Australia, and I've seen it across the world in less fortunate environments. I work as part of the International Burns Society where we have a mantra: one world, one standard of burn care. It's an aspirational goal we strive towards, by sharing our knowledge, our energy and our time.

'I believe in goodness in people, and I think that is what we need to harness. We need to harness the positive energy, and we need to do so such that our science and technology of the future shines. So that we can leave a history behind us that we are proud of.'

Fiona is now recognised as one of Australia's National Living Treasures. She has never stopped striving to improve and evolve the treatment of burns patients – and to spread the power of positivity in our world.

National Living Treasures

In 1997 the National Trust of Australia founded the National Living Treasures of Australia: 100 living Australians are nominated and voted onto the list for making a substantial and enduring contribution to Australian society.

Burns first aid

In a fire

Stop, drop and roll: Drop to the ground, cover your face, and roll away from the flames. This will help smother the fire.

Burn first aid

1. Remove wet clothing and jewellery.

2. Cool the injury for 20 minutes under cold running water. If you don't have running water, wet two cloths and place them on the burn, alternating every two minutes.

3. Cover the injury loosely with a clean wet cloth or towel.

4. Keep the patient warm.

5. Seek medical assistance.

The Fiona Wood Foundation is dedicated to improving outcomes for people with burns. For more information or to help support the Fiona Wood Foundation's life-saving work, please visit www.fionawoodfoundation.com.

Glossary

▷ **biology:** a branch of science that deals with the study of life. A biologist might study the structure, function, growth, origin and evolution of living organisms.

▷ **cadaver:** a dead human body used by medical students and physicians for study purposes.

▷ **cell culture:** the process by which cells are grown under controlled conditions, like in a lab.

▷ **cell differentiation:** a process where young cells begin to change and distinguish themselves from other cells.

▷ **clinical trial:** research experiment where people volunteer to test new treatments for various medical conditions.

▷ **enzymes:** proteins that help speed up chemical reactions in our bodies, without being permanently changed themselves.

▷ **formalin:** a clear liquid solution used to preserve specimens and as an antiseptic and disinfectant.

▷ **foundling:** an infant that has been abandoned by its parents and found and cared for by others.

▷ **pit head:** the top of a mining pit or coal shaft.

- **Quakers:** this religious group does not have formal ceremonies or systems of belief; instead they believe that everyone has inward access to God and therefore we are all spiritually equal.

- **scholarship:** money awarded to a student to help pay for their education. Usually given based on academic or extra-curricular achievement.

- **skin graft:** surgical operation where a piece of healthy skin is transplanted to an injured area of skin to help it heal.

- **spoil heaps:** a pile for stacking waste material removed during mining.

- **terrorist:** someone who uses unlawful violence against a society they don't agree with, in an attempt to achieve political goals.

- **triage nurse:** when a patient comes into the emergency room, a triage nurse is the one who first assesses them to decide what they need.

About Cristy Burne

Cristy Burne grew up climbing trees, jumping drains, chasing runaway cows and inventing stories. Before she became a writer, she was science circus performer, garbage analyst, Santa's pixie and an English teacher.

Currently Cristy is a children's author, science writer and presenter. She has worked as a science communicator in the US, UK, Japan, South Africa, Switzerland and Australia, editing science magazines and contributing to children's STEM publications, including CSIRO's *Double Helix* and *Scientriffic*.

Cristy's books are published in three languages. She has a passion for STEM, loves learning through doing, and aims to inspire creativity, daring and resilience in her readers.